Schooling
a Young Horse
by George Wheatley

Published by
Melvin Powers
WILSHIRE BOOK COMPANY
12015 Sherman Road
No. Hollywood, California 91605
Telephone: (213) 875-1711 / (818) 983-1105

By the same author
STABLE MANAGEMENT FOR THE OWNER-GROOM

Drawings by Mary Gernatt
Photography by Major P. O'Connor

© George Wheatley 1968. First American edition published 1968 by
A. S. Barnes and Company, Inc., Cranbury, New Jersey 08512.

Library of Congress Catalogue Card Number: 68-29868

ISBN 0-87980-201-4

6973
PRINTED IN THE UNITED STATES OF AMERICA

*To my pupils, 'Tarquin' and his owner, Caroline,
in acknowledgement of the happy hours which she and I have spent in
schooling him. With best wishes for their future partnership*

CONTENTS

1 The Foal

There stands our young foal, with the innocence, beauty, gaiety and appealing charm of all young creatures. What does its future hold? That is entirely in our hands. It is our responsibility, as its owner, to form, create and mould its temperament, character and action.

A young foal

Its future trust and confidence in humanity depend upon our handling, particularly in the earliest stages. Therefore, ideally, only one person should handle the foal right from birth, so that it may acquire complete confidence and trust. Nobody else should be allowed to touch or feed it. This applies throughout the whole period of its training, especially later when it has been backed and starts being schooled. Only its trainer should then ride the young horse until it is thoroughly schooled and really understands and implicitly obeys the aids. As no two people ride alike any slightly different application of the aids could upset and confuse a young horse. And even a mature, well-schooled horse can quickly be ruined by a bad rider, with a bad seat and hands, or an inexperienced one who allows the horse to have its own way, whether in the stable or when being ridden. A horse very quickly knows when it is being handled or ridden by someone who is timid or inexperienced and will 'play up' accordingly—like a child.

The secret lies in gentleness, the whole time, and infinite patience, combined with firmness and a complete lack of fear, or at any rate the ability not to show it or let the horse become aware of it. This also necessitates a knowledge and understanding of horse psychology: one must try to understand the way its mind works and the natural instincts which govern its behaviour.

For instance, horses are naturally inclined to be jealous. Watch their reactions and behaviour towards each other at feeding-time, when those which are normally perfectly friendly will turn round and bite, or let out with their heels if they think that another horse is receiving more food or attention than they are, or that another horse is going to steal their food.

Horses are timid by nature. Their natural defence lies in speed of flight—which is why a frightened horse tries to bolt. If cornered they will defend themselves by biting, or by turning round and kicking.

Stallions, by nature, are more prone to rear up and strike out with their forelegs, as they do when fighting for the supremacy of their mares. Two stallions fighting for a mare will rear up and attack each other with their teeth and forelegs.

Mares are more prone to kick out with their hindlegs and are likely to be uncertain in temperament, especially when in season.

A horse's other natural instinct is its search for food. It grazes intermittently for about twenty hours out of the twenty-four; it only sleeps for about four hours, and then often while standing up, and ready for instant flight if suddenly alarmed.

Few horses are wicked or vicious by nature. Most so-called 'vices' are the result of bad handling at some time or other. Many are caused by mishandling as a foal; its natural trust has been turned to distrust by impatient or rough handling.

Take rearing, for example. If one tries to drag an unwilling foal forward it naturally resists by trying to pull back, and if one is impatient and tries to apply force it instinctively tries to escape by rearing up. The seeds of one 'vice' have been sown. From that time on, whenever the foal wants to resist it will try to back away and rear.

Again, the habit of nipping, which originates by giving the young foal too many indiscriminate titbits, or by allowing it to search in one's pockets for food, can result in the more serious vice of biting. Young things are so attractive and it is all too easy to spoil them. The youngster learns to expect a titbit every time it sees its owner; if not given one, it shows temper and resentment by trying to nip. Or maybe it is just sheer anxiety to receive the expected dainty. Prevention is better than cure: titbits should be reserved only for catching, turning out, or as a reward for something special, for example, at the end of a lesson, for good behaviour.

Like a young child, a foal learns to respect and appreciate gentle, yet firm and consistent discipline. Allowing it to get away with murder at one time and then punishing it, perhaps for the same fault, at another, according to one's mood at the moment, only makes it feel insecure, and sows the seeds of doubt, and uncertainty. Punishment should never depend upon the owner's temper, whim or mood. It should rarely be necessary. If it has to be meted out it should be administered calmly and immediately. Then the foal can be made to understand what it has done wrong, and it shows no resentment at being scolded.

Besides being timid, a horse is naturally gentle and anxious to please. So, coaxing and rewarding it (a pat on the neck or a kindly-spoken word—not necessarily always food) should be the main approach. One's tone of voice is a most valuable asset in all training and schooling. It can soothe, encourage, reward or frighten. A horse also quickly learns to understand and obey simple verbal commands such as 'Whoa' (or 'Stand'), 'Walk', 'Trot', etc. 'Steady' is one of the most useful words of command both in and out of the stable. The foal should be taught to understand it from the start.

I dislike the term usually used of 'breaking' a young horse, which, to me, seems to imply destroying something. Surely what we want to do is to educate step by step, to create, not to 'break' a young horse's spirit? The aim in training a young foal from the earliest stages should be to make and develop gradually an animal of grace and beauty, and to ensure that it gives generous service. We are trying to build and form (or mould) its character, and later, to develop its muscles and natural conformation, to make the best of whatever it is inherently capable of becoming. If a foal has been well-handled and well-disciplined and is accustomed to obeying the voice from the earliest stages, and later is accustomed to being groomed and to having its head and legs handled, and has been taught good stable manners, then the whole process will have been so gentle and gradual that it is simply a question of education, introducing it progressively to new ideas and experiences. Still later, its education will consist of learning a language of signs which both it and its rider will understand when the time comes for it to be backed and ridden. If it has complete confidence in the person schooling it, it will be ready and willing to learn. And the habit of obedience will already have been established.

A horse is not generally rated as particularly high in intelligence, though personally I feel that it understands a good deal more than we believe it does. Nevertheless a horse's reactions are largely instinctive, governed by fear of the unknown, and desire for food. A horse is capable of a limited amount of affection for its owner, if well treated, merely because it regards him as the bringer of food and other comforts of its existence. But, if treated kindly, made comfortable and fed well, a horse will soon settle down quite happily with a new owner, in new surroundings. Unlike a cat it evinces no apparent desire to return to its former home, though it may recognize its old surroundings if it ever goes back to them, even years later. It will also recognize its former owner and even show signs of pleasure at seeing him again.

One valuable asset a horse has is a very long, retentive memory. It never forgets, especially rough handling, and will attack a former groom who has treated it badly, with ears back and teeth bared, if it meets him again.

Coupled with its retentive memory is a horse's liking for a regular routine. It likes things being done every day at the same time and in the same order, and soon begins to know its daily schedule. For instance, if horses out at grass are always fed at the same time, they will fidget and fuss and start milling round if their owner is late. They will congregate at the fence or gate and trouble usually starts if one is unpunctual. A horse seems to have an instinctive 'clock' in its head. Again, if always fed in a certain part of its field, a horse will go to that place when it sees its owner approaching with a bowl of food.

This time sense and liking for a regular ordered routine can be used as valuable assets in training and schooling, both in and out of the stable. In the stable a regular routine will be useful in teaching the foal good stable manners, and in accustoming it to being groomed, and having its legs handled and its feet picked up, as a valuable preparation for being shod; if the same order of procedure is always followed it soon learns to know what to expect. Similarly in training it, say, to being led, it will learn more quickly if one adopts the same procedure at each lesson.

In training, each new step must be thoroughly understood, and once the horse has understood what is required, the lesson must be given time to sink in thoroughly. It should be repeated sufficiently often until it is remembered and has become a habit.

Many a potentially good young horse has been soured and permanently ruined in temperament, and performance, through impatience and the forcing on of its earliest training as a foal. In fact this applies throughout at all stages of schooling.

It takes four years to make and school a young horse, in its elementary training, up to the time that it is backed, ridden and taught the aids—and four weeks for a bad rider to ruin a well-schooled horse.

The foal's early feeding after being weaned is of the utmost importance. Unless it has a good start in the first year of its life, its whole future physical development can be retarded and even stunted. After weaning, give food of the best quality, and plenty of it. Besides the best hay obtainable give it at least three short feeds daily, consisting of crushed oats mixed with linseed jelly. Also small doses of cod-liver oil for developing bone and muscle. Once a week give it a warm bran mash, especially in winter. In winter add a small quantity of carrot, apple and root vegetables, such as swedes or turnips, to the feeds; the two latter are especially valuable in cold weather. Carrots, apples and root vegetables must be cut up really small (never diced, as they may stick in the foal's throat and choke it); cutting vegetables into really small pieces and mixing them with some dry bran, or chaff, prevents the foal from bolting its food and giving itself indigestion, and possibly colic. Bran mash is a mild laxative, while dry bran has the opposite effect.

As the horse has a small stomach, for its size, and a large intestine, and needs to have a certain amount of food constantly passing through the digestive organs, short feeds only are insufficient. It needs a certain amount of bulk or 'roughage', which hay provides. Also, the same quantity of short feed is better given in smaller, more frequent feeds than in larger ones given less frequently: five feeds per day are better than four, if possible, while four are better than three, although the total amount of food given is the same.

A foal will begin sharing its mother's feed when about three weeks old. This should be encouraged as it will mean less difficulty when the foal is weaned. Spread out the food in a low trough or manger, and increase the amount, otherwise the mare may push the foal away.

When it is turned out (and it should be allowed to graze as soon as possible), the foal will begin to imitate its mother by nibbling at the grass at a very early age. Be careful that the grass is not too rich and lush, otherwise it may upset the foal's digestion and give it colic.

It can be put out by itself, when the mare is taken out for exercise, in a movable pen made of hurdles. Thus in fine weather it can learn to graze and can exercise itself by day. The pen's position should be changed frequently—never leave it in hot sunshine or in a cold wind. Provide a bucket of clean water; a foal will drink as soon as it can reach it. When first parted from its mother, it will probably protest with heart-rending shrieks and the mare may not want to leave it. Making her leave her foal and accustoming it to graze alone for an hour or so is again good preparation for eventual weaning.

Never allow the foal to suckle when the mare is tired, or hot and sweating, as this can cause a skin irritation which is difficult to cure.

The foal will be ready for weaning after it is about six or seven months old. Do not allow it to run with its mother for too long. One indication that the time has come for them to part is that the mare will start trying to repulse the foal when it attempts to suckle. Weaning takes about a week; there should be an absolutely clean break and the foal should be completely separated so that they are out of sight of each other. Give the foal a companion to distract its attention, another foal of its own age if possible, but failing that a donkey or small calf will do.

After the separation, the mare should be partially milked out on the next morning, and the following day if necessary, but not too frequently or she will not go dry. Keep her on dry feeds and best quality old hay, turning her out onto rather bare pasture until she has dried off. Do not let her graze on rich grass. Applying black treacle to the teats helps the drying-off process.

Changing over from liquid to solid diet almost invariably affects the foal's condition, and it tends to lose flesh. It may also become hidebound and pot-bellied.

It should be dosed for worms at about eight months old as a precaution. The modern method for worming is to use 'Equizole' pellets or cubes. This does away with the old-fashioned process of worming—keeping the foal without water and then purging. It was a complicated, tiresome business, and purging was very likely to upset the foal's digestive system, and/or cause colic. One simply mixes Equizole pellets in the feed and they are supposed to eradicate all types of worms. Consult the makers regarding dosage for a foal, or follow your veterinary surgeon's advice.

Field shelter—note wide entrance. PHOTO SUPPLIED BY EDWARDS AND SON (MALMESBURY) LTD

Adequate shelter is a necessity, especially during the first year of a foal's life. A shelter should provide protection against cold north and east winds, and can take the form of high, really thick hedges or a high wall; preferably a field shelter should be erected. If there is inadequate shelter the foal must be brought inside in hot sun or cold winds. It is not perhaps generally realized that horses are susceptible to sunstroke. Those comic straw hats worn by horses, donkeys and mules in Mediterranean countries are not merely provided for the amusement of tourists.

Encourage the foal to use the field shelter by putting its feed inside, and by providing a good deep bed of wheat straw on which it can lie down. Keep the shelter floor clean and free from droppings and sodden straw to avoid foot troubles.

In very severe weather bring the foal in at night, particularly when there is a likelihood of freezing rain. One does not want to make one's horse soft, but one must use one's discretion. Cold weather, even snow, certainly does no harm, provided the foal has adequate shelter, plenty of good food and a thick winter coat: icy rain, followed by a freezing wind, can kill. On the other hand, stabled horses or ponies are more prone to coughs, colds and other ailments, because they lead an artificial life, while those that live out have a much harder existence. Thoroughbreds should not be left to live out.

A field shelter should face towards the south or west and should be sited in a sheltered corner of the field. It will also be used during the day in summer, as a protection against flies, particularly horse-flies, or midges in the evening, and in very hot sunshine. It is quite a good thing to allow cobwebs to accumulate in the corners as they entangle the flies.

The shelter should have a wide opening; a narrow one is dangerous if it is used by more than one animal, in case there is a kicking match.

As already advised, a foal should be handled from birth if possible, and always by the same person.

For the first few days, take advantage of its natural friendliness and inquisitiveness. Very young creatures seem to have little fear of man; it is only later that they become suspicious and apprehensive, through experience. Encourage the foal to come to you and very gently try to fondle and stroke it, to gain its confidence. Be very slow and quiet in movement as it is easily startled. Accustom it to the sound of your voice from the beginning. If it tends to be shy and timid smear a little treacle on your finger and let it suck it off, until it will come to you of its own accord.

Some mares are very jealous and suspicious and will not allow one to approach their foal; they will hustle it away and stand guard before it with an anxious look, and may even attack one. So, be careful! In this case it is better to bring the mare into the stable and tie her up before trying to handle the foal. It will naturally follow its mother when she is led into the stable.

Handling and controlling a foal

Having tied her up in a box and shut the door so that the foal cannot enter, coax the foal to you. If the mare is tied up in a stall keep well out of reach of her heels. It is unsafe to approach the foal when its mother is loose in the paddock as she may charge at you, neck outstretched, with ears back and teeth bared, or she may suddenly swing round and let out with her heels.

Not all mares are possessive in this way; some will acquiesce and stand and watch with maternal pride and approval, while you entice and make much of their offspring.

Discourage visitors very firmly: only the person in charge should be allowed near the mare and foal for at least several weeks. And only one person should handle the foal. An admiring crowd always clustered around is unsettling for both, especially as the majority of visitors, particularly youngsters, will persist in trying to feed and pet the foal. I knew of one lovely foal that was literally killed by kindness; it died through overfeeding by all and sundry who insisted on coming to see it.

One advantage of being able to handle the foal from birth, or when only a few days old, is that one is stronger than it is. The foal quickly realizes this and it inculcates a feeling of healthy respect in its infantile mind.

Catching a foal

To catch a foal, put your left hand round under its throat and your right arm around its hindquarters below its tail. Hold it in the same way, left hand under its neck and right arm round its buttocks. It can also be lifted up and carried, with hands and arms in the same position. Accustom it to being caught, held and carried, by doing so several times daily.

Carrying a foal

After it is a week to a fortnight old and has been handled daily, accustom it to wearing a foal-slip (head-collar). But if it still tries to struggle when being handled, postpone this next step until it has quietened down. At all costs try to avoid any fuss the first time the foal-slip is put on, or the foal will be frightened and will lose the trust it has already gained in you. Once there is a struggle in which one uses force, it will resist wearing the foal-slip every time one tries to put it on; it will probably make it head-shy and may make it difficult, later, to bridle.

Leave the slip on only for a few minutes the first time it is worn. Put it on several times during the first day. While it is wearing the slip, make much of the foal, and encourage it with your voice, let it suck treacle off your finger, or feed it with tiny pieces of sugar. This will distract its attention from the whole bewildering, unpleasant business, and it will also begin to associate the wearing of the slip with something pleasant.

A foal-slip

After a few days, when accustomed to having the slip put on, and to wearing it for gradually increasing periods, the next step is to teach it to follow when led. It will probably try to resist at first, planting all four feet firmly on the ground and refusing to move an inch, or it may try to pull back. Let an assistant lead the mare slowly in front, away from it; the foal will probably try to follow its mother, especially if it thinks it is going to be left behind. Once it moves it can be led several times round the yard, following the mare.

First lessons in being led should be given on soft ground, or in a straw-covered yard, where the foal cannot hurt itself if it resists and falls, or if it throws itself down, as it may do. If a foal can fall over and hurt itself, it most certainly will; so make quite sure that no obstacles are near, such as heaps of stones, stable implements, wooden planks,

Leading a mare, with her young foal following

buckets, or anything, in fact, against which it could possibly hit and injure itself, or in which it could get its legs entangled. A foal's legs are very easily broken because they are so long.

If it refuses to move, have its mother led slowly away; at the same time another assistant should push it gently along from behind. Also, have a long, thin switch in your hand and very gently stroke or tap its hindquarters until it moves forward. Directly it shows signs of moving reward it by letting it suck treacle off your fingers. Take plenty of time and have infinite patience; above all, never allow it to develop into a struggle which will frighten and bewilder the foal and again destroy its confidence. Never try to drag it forward by sheer brute force. As you are the stronger one you may ultimately succeed, but meanwhile, the more you pull the more the foal will resist and try to pull back, and it will try to rear up in its efforts to escape. It will try this same evasion each time until it has formed the habit of rearing. And once it has done so it will be very difficult to cure. First lessons should be very short—only about ten to fifteen minutes.

When it has learnt to be led and it follows easily, it can be taken for short walks with its mother, also being led, following behind her.

It can also be led out for exercise on days when the weather is too uncertain for it to be left out in its pen to graze and exercise itself.

When teaching the foal to lead it is very important from the beginning to inculcate the idea and habit of free forward movement, as this forms the basis of impulsion in all future schooling. That is another reason why it should never be dragged, but always pushed forward from behind. All forward movement and impulsion must come from the hindquarters.

Result of trying to drag a foal forward—teaching it to rear

So the first idea to inculcate is that of free forward movement, from the very first lesson in being led. Obedience should be insisted upon from the beginning. The foal should also be taught to obey simple verbal commands, starting with 'Stand' or 'Whoa', 'Walk on', and 'Steady', when it tries to play up. Having learnt to recognize and obey these it can be taught the meaning of 'Back'. But in teaching it to move back, one must again be careful, as it may try to rear up when backed. This must not be allowed and must be checked immediately by making the foal move forward.

When given the command to 'Stand', insist on the foal standing still for at least a minute, or until it is told to move forward again. One may have to ask an assistant to hold it at first. Similarly it should be made to slow up and stop immediately when one says 'Whoa'. Again, ask your helper to walk quietly by its head and stop it moving forward directly you give the order.

These orders should be taught one at a time so that there is no confusion in the foal's mind. They must each be repeated frequently until the sound of the word has been associated with the appropriate action. Directly it shows signs of recognition and obedience, reward the foal and make much of it. Always use the same tone of voice and way of giving a command; for instance, do not say 'W-a-a-l-k' one day, and then 'Walk', or 'Walk on', the next. Allow a short interval of time for the foal to react, and for the reflex muscular response to follow the sound of the word. At first its reflexes will be slow. But gradually, as the foal learns to recognize the sound of the word and forms the habit of obedience, the reflex response will become quicker, until eventually it will become an automatic reaction. Some horses will always respond more slowly than others, just as one human being's reflexes are slower than another's.

The next stage is to accustom the foal to being tied up and left by itself. Having been accustomed to its freedom hitherto, it may at first resent this; also, it may not like being left completely alone, although it should be more or less used to this if it has been put out in a pen to graze by itself. But still, being tied up by itself in a stable is rather a different matter.

Lead it into a stall and tie it up. Then retreat out of sight, but keep near so that you can untie it quickly, in case the foal tries to pull back or starts to throw itself about. When it stands quietly for a few minutes reward and make much of it. For the first few times that it is tied up and left, give it a small feed to occupy its attention. Directly it has finished eating reappear and untie it. Repeat this several times daily until it becomes used to being tied up and left alone. Gradually increase the length of time it is tied up.

This training can be combined with practice in leading the foal in hand, by itself, in and out of the stable. Also, continue the lessons in obedience to vocal commands, 'Whoa', 'Stand', 'Walk on', 'Turn', and so on. Gradually add to the foal's vocabulary. For instance, when accustomed to being tied up in the stable, teach it to understand what 'Move over' means. This will form the basis of teaching it good stable manners.

3 Discipline

As soon as the foal has accepted the idea of being tied up in the stable, one can take the first steps towards accustoming it to being groomed by gently stroking it all over with one's hand.

However, some foals object strongly to being handled and will not allow one to stroke or brush them in any way. In that case, first try stroking the foal very gently with a soft pad attached to a long pole, so that you do not have to go near it, and rub it along its back and over its hindquarters. Stop at once if the foal appears to be frightened. Speak soothingly to it and reward it immediately the first time it allows itself to be touched and stroked. When it finally allows you to stroke it with the pad attached to the pole, and has become used to this, then try to persuade it to allow you to stroke it with your hand. Do not try stroking its head with the pad, in case it jerks its head and is knocked by the pole. It can so easily be made head-shy, through being frightened by an accidental knock.

Handling a foal's legs

The foal's legs should also be handled daily in the stable. Run your hand very slowly and lightly down each leg from shoulder to fetlock. Always speak first, and when it allows you to handle its legs, reward it with a titbit.

When it will stand quietly while you run your hand down its legs, then hold its fetlock and try to make the foal lift up its foot. Say 'Up' or 'Foot' each time as you do so. Again, reward it immediately it allows its foot to be raised off the ground. If it steadfastly refuses, gently pinch its tendons at the fetlock between your finger and thumb, and push your shoulder against the foal to over-balance it, so that it has to move its leg. Again, at the same time say 'Up' or 'Foot'.

Handling and picking up feet

This may take some time to achieve, and great tact and patience are necessary. Some horses will pick their feet up easily, while others are invariably difficult, probably due to bad early training. Never try to force the foal to lift up its foot, or engage in a struggle with it. This is a new idea to it, which it has to understand and become accustomed to; eventually it will allow you to run your hand down its leg and pick up its foot when told.

When the foal will allow you to touch and handle its body and legs, try brushing it very gently all over with a soft brush (a baby's hair-brush will answer the purpose very well). Rest one hand on the foal when brushing its body, and when brushing its legs hold the leg in one hand whilst brushing with the other. On no account use a dandy-brush as a foal's skin is very tender. A water-brush with soft hairs will be suitable, as the first step after the baby's hair-brush; then gradually accustom it to a body-brush. Be especially careful when grooming the head, or any ticklish spots such as underneath the belly, the flanks, or inside the hindlegs.

Handling its legs and teaching it to lift up its feet is in preparation for the day when it first has its feet trimmed by the blacksmith. And, as far as this is concerned, it is most important to have a blacksmith who is patient, sympathetic and gentle, yet firm. Any struggle or rough, impatient handling may result in the foal being permanently difficult to shoe.

If a horse has been properly trained and handled it should never be

Catching—approaching with foal-slip over left arm and titbit in left hand

difficult to catch. All mine eventually have always come to call. In fact they will often even canter across the field towards me, when they see me coming and hear my call. There is nothing more exasperating, or time wasting, than a horse or pony that refuses to be caught.

So, train the foal from the very first time that it is turned out. Go down armed with a titbit, call the foal and persuade it to come to you. Directly it does so, reward it; let it suck treacle off your fingers, or give it tiny pieces of lump sugar, or a small piece of bread. The natural inquisitiveness and friendliness of the young will probably make it come up to you in the first instance, and directly it discovers that it is rewarded with something pleasant, it will quickly learn to come trotting up whenever it sees you, especially if you always call to it in the same way as you approach its pen. Never allow it to try to search in your pockets for food, and if in its anxiety to have the expected titbit it tries to nibble your fingers or nip, scold it kindly but firmly with your voice and give it a little tap on the nose, saying 'No' as you do so. It will not become afraid or show resentment, once it understands that taking liberties, such as nipping or searching in pockets, are not allowed; and it will soon learn to respect you.

When trying to catch the foal, never shout at it or wave your arms about. If it turns away, never make a sudden grab at it, or chase after it. You may teach it the habit of kicking if it is startled, and if chased it will only think that it is a game. It will then become permanently difficult to catch.

Do not attempt to put on the foal-slip for the first few times. When the foal has learnt to come up to you when called, then take the slip with you. Let it approach you in the usual way and hold a titbit in the palm of your left hand, with the slip hanging ready on your outstretched arm. As the foal takes the titbit from your left hand, turn very slowly and face in the same direction. Then very quietly try to slide your right arm gently under its neck while it is eating. If it is startled or tries to back away desist immediately and give it another titbit. When its confidence is once more restored, try again. You may not succeed the first day that you attempt this, but do the same thing daily, several times a day, until the foal eventually allows you to slip your right arm under its neck. Then very quietly, but quickly, drop the foal-slip over its nose with your left hand, keeping your right hand ready to put the strap over its neck to be buckled. After this there should be no further difficulty.

Putting on foal-slip

When turning the foal out into its pen, lead it in and close the entrance. Then lead it forward several yards and turn it round to face the entrance. Before unfastening the foal-slip, make it stand still for a minute or two while you fondle it and give it a titbit. Then unbuckle the slip and walk quietly away. Adopt the same procedure when turning it out, so that it becomes a fixed habit for it to stand still and wait until released. This will also prevent it from learning the dangerous habits, which some horses have, of trying to turn round and break away directly it enters its field, or of turning round and flinging up its heels before galloping off. In either case one may easily get kicked. Also, never give it a slap on the hindquarters or wave your arms about to make it canter off. The last impression left on its mind will influence its behaviour next time you want to catch it.

4 Stable Manners

Our young foal's training is progressing, and already in the first months of its life it has learnt many valuable lessons. Now its training in stable manners should be continued.

Stable manners—short-racking

Accustom the foal next to the idea of being short-racked, i.e., being tied up on a short rope for grooming or any other special purpose, so that it cannot turn round, or back away. It may at first resent this new interference with its liberty, by trying to pull back directly it feels the rope being shortened. So do not tie the rope with a quick-release knot for the first few times; merely shorten the rope gradually, a little more each time, and hold it for a minute or so. Every time the foal accepts this and does not try to back away, and stands still when short-racked, make much of it with your voice and give it a pat on the neck or a titbit.

If it tries to pull back do not try to keep the rope short but let it gradually slide through the tie-ring and lengthen. Do not have the tie-ring too high so that the foal's head aad neck are pulled up into a constrained and unnatural position. Repeat this short-racking daily, several times a day, for as long as necessary until the foal accepts it and has learnt the lesson. When it has, try tying it with a quick-release knot for a short period. Stand by in readiness to unfasten the rope if the foal begins to struggle or pull back. Try never to allow any part of its training to degenerate into a fight against authority. Willing co-operation is always one's aim.

By now the foal will have grown considerably and one will no longer be able to pick it up and carry it. The foal is the stronger of the two; in fact it is probably strong enough to make even two powerful men look rather foolish if it came to a trial of strength. So one must avoid a fight in which it will realize its own greater strength. Once it does realize this, it will try to make use of the fact to rebel against one's authority.

When the foal has learnt to stand still whilst short-racked, you can safely take it to have its feet trimmed for the first time.

At two months old it will be possible to form a pretty shrewd idea as to the foal's future looks and conformation. If it looks well-balanced and smart, then it will probably make a good horse, however plain its appearance may become whilst growing up. Like a young adolescent human it will probably go through a gawky stage, but, in stable language, it will 'return to its foal form'.

At about six months old the colt (or filly), as it is now, will be weaned and ready to begin the first stages of its formal education. If properly handled up to this time, it should cause little trouble and will hardly need 'breaking' in the normally accepted sense of the word.

A few hints on handling horses in general also apply to handling the colt. Talk to it as to a child and whistle about the place as you work. Horses like someone with a cheerful disposition, and in general like the sound of the human voice and are greatly influenced by it. Never shout at it, but speak and move about quietly. Avoid making un-necessary or sudden noises, such as slamming doors or clattering buckets, which may startle it, or upset a highly strung colt's nerves. Thoroughbreds are much more 'nervy' than, say, native British breeds of pony. The more 'aristocratic' a horse is, the more highly strung and temperamental it is likely to be.

While grooming be very careful not to hit it with the back of the brush. And be careful not to knock it with the metal curry comb, if this is held in your other hand ready for cleaning dust out of the brush. Most horses hate being patted on the face or forehead, and will jerk or turn away their heads and blink. Never come up suddenly from behind and give it a hearty slap on its hindquarters; always speak before approaching to warn it, whether you are coming from in front or from behind.

Most horses (unless they have been made head-shy), love having their ears gently pulled through one's fingers, called 'stripping'; this also helps to warm them when they are feeling cold. One can tell if a horse is cold by feeling the base of its ears: if the roots of its ears are cold the horse is cold. Horses also like being rubbed under their jowl and will stand quietly with a rapt expression of contentment for as long as one likes to do it. It is a good way of calming down a startled horse, especially if one talks soothingly to it at the same time. They like, too, having the top of their head and their cheeks rubbed gently. If a horse is nervous do not bring your hand down onto its head from above, but raise it slowly upwards from below. Fondling a colt in these ways will have a soothing effect on it.

It is now time for the colt to have its first shoes. The importance of employing a quiet, patient blacksmith has already been stressed. I have met blacksmiths who shout at the horse or poke it in the belly, or even hit it in the ribs with the handle of their hammer. It is worse than useless employing such a man to shoe a nervous colt for the first time, however expert his actual shoeing may be.

If the colt has already had its feet trimmed regularly up to now, it will know the blacksmith and will have confidence in him, which is half the battle; so being shod for the first time should cause little trouble. It is already thoroughly accustomed to having its legs handled and its feet picked up.

Stand by, ready to help soothe the colt and talk to it if necessary. Sometimes dangling a bunch of keys in front will distract its attention. The jangling appears to be the attraction. I once successfully used this method with an excitable young racehorse which, until then, had succeeded in resisting all the blacksmith's, and the stable lad's, efforts to touch its feet. Standing by with a bowl of oats, pieces of carrot, or other favourite titbit, also usually effectively takes its mind off this new and bewildering experience of being shod.

But unless you want permanent trouble and difficulty, at all costs try to avoid a 'scene' at this first shoeing. If the colt is being 'hot shod', as it should be, the smoke, when the hot shoe is applied to its foot, may upset it. That is when tactful intervention with some food may prevent trouble: keep its attention occupied somehow during the process.

As part of its formal education, after the age of about six months, one can start 'mouthing' the colt. On no account try to force the bit into its mouth. Once it mentally associates wearing the bit with an unpleasant experience it will refuse to take it, and it is most annoying, and time wasting, to have a daily struggle with a horse which refuses to open its mouth and accept the bit.

Use a mouthing-bit when first introducing the colt to the idea of having something in its mouth. This has loose pendants or 'keys' attached to the bit, which may be made of rubber, vulcanite or metal; rubber or vulcanite are the softest and encourage the colt to play with the bit. The keys will also make it play with the bit, and they encourage the formation of saliva. This helps to 'make' its mouth, and keeps it soft.

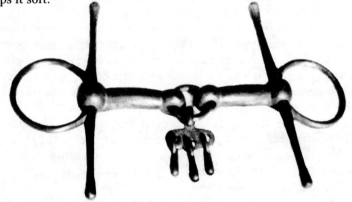

Metal mouthing-bit with 'keys'

The first time you introduce the mouthing-bit to the colt smear the bar and the keys with something sweet—black treacle does very well. Show it the bit first and let it sniff at and lick it. Once it discovers the treacle and likes the taste, it will try to lick it off. This is the appropriate moment, while the colt is licking its lips, to slip the bit into its mouth.

At first the bit should be attached to the head-collar which it is accustomed to wearing; it should be adjusted to rest comfortably between the bars of the mouth. The colt will chew happily at the bit and play with the keys in its efforts to lick off the treacle, and will froth at the mouth. The first time it is worn remove the bit after about ten to fifteen minutes, or as soon as it has successfully licked off all the treacle.

Always apply treacle for the first few times that the bit is worn; soon the colt will begin to look for, and eagerly accept, the bit in anticipation of the pleasant taste. I used this method effectively to cure a pony I had bought which refused to take the bit. It soon looked for it and putting on the bridle became a pleasure for us both, instead of an exasperating struggle. The only trouble was that when it came to unbridling, the pony was loth to part with his bit! Needless to say there is no treacle on the bit now; but he still eagerly looks for it and drops his head, with his mouth open ready to receive it.

Gradually increase the length of time during which the bit is in the colt's mouth. Let it wear it two or three times daily in its box, until eventually it is left in, say, for two hours in the morning and an hour in the afternoon.

During the later stages substitute an ordinary straight-barred rubber or vulcanite, or sometimes a plain jointed, or an egg-butt, snaffle. The bar of the bit should be fairly thick, as this is milder and more comfortable than a thinner one (see page 47).

This training, combined with continued training in stable manners, daily handling and practice in being led whilst walking or trotting, should complete the foal's first year.

5 The Colt : Second and Third Years

The colt's training in stable manners should now be well advanced. It should be thoroughly accustomed to being tied up and left, and to being short-racked while being groomed. It should stand quietly and be perfectly amenable to being groomed all over, and to lifting up its feet to have them picked out. It should obey quite quickly when told to stand, move over, turn or back in its box as required.

Lungeing—first stage: being led by assistant

While being mouthed it can also start learning to be lunged. The first stage is to begin lungeing it in a head-collar, without a bit in its mouth. It has already learnt to move forward freely while being led, at a walk and trot, and must now be introduced to the idea of free forward movement in a circle, while being lunged. It must also now learn to obey verbal commands to stand, walk on or trot on, given by the person lungeing it. Being lunged also teaches it to balance itself correctly at the walk and trot, and it develops its muscles. The canter comes considerably later when it is moving freely and obediently on the lunge-rein.

Let an assistant lead the colt in a circle, while you stand in the middle. Use a one-inch broad-tape lungeing-rein, about eighteen feet long, attached to the front of a cavesson noseband with a swivel ring; this is fitted to a special lungeing head-collar. Or, better still, fasten the lungeing-rein to the back of the noseband underneath the horse's chin, thus avoiding any pull or jab on its sensitive nose.

When you give the order 'W-a-a-l-k', or 'Walk on', whichever you normally use, your assistant should lead the colt forward. Stand in the centre just level with the colt's hindquarters, and make it circle in front of you on a fairly short lunge-rein, but sufficient to be out of reach of its heels.

When circling to the left hold the lunge-rein in your left hand with your arm extended outwards in the direction of the colt's movement, and the lungeing-whip in your right hand. While the colt is standing still keep the whip pointing downwards to the ground, so as not to startle it: do not flourish the whip about with its lash waving in the air.

As soon as you give the order to walk trail the whiplash just off the ground behind the colt's hindquarters. If it is sluggish or disobedient and refuses to walk forward, very lightly flick its hock or its hindquarters with the lash, at the same time repeating the order to walk on.

Stand still in the centre and make the colt move round you in a circle. Do not wander about, but turn round more or less on the same spot.

When the colt is circling at a walk with your assistant holding its head-collar, on the outside of the circle, give the order to stop. I personally prefer saying 'Stand' and 'Walk on', as 'Whoa' sounds very like 'Walk' and may therefore cause confusion. Circle round several times, alternately giving the orders to 'Stand' and 'Walk on'. Then change the direction and repeat for an equal number of times on the opposite circle. If the colt has been circling to the left, transfer the lungeing-rein to your right hand and the whip to your left hand, when circling to the right. Never lunge the whole time on the same circle as this makes a horse one-sided, developing its muscles more on one side than the other.

The whip shaft should be about six feet long and should have a long, thin flexible lash (or thong); when the colt is standing still, or when changing direction keep the lash looped up in your hand, with the whip pointing to the ground.

As soon as the colt understands what is required of it and begins to obey your orders to 'Walk on' and 'Stand', ask your assistant to walk by its head without actually holding the head-collar.

Lungeing—final stage: without any assistant

The final stage is for the colt to circle in both directions, walking and stopping when told, by itself without anyone walking by its head. When it can do this, gradually lengthen the rein as it circles.

The next step is to teach the colt to trot on the lunge, without 'hotting up' or becoming excited. It may be necessary to invoke your assistant's help again, asking him to lead the colt round at a walk, and then at a trot when you give the appropriate orders. If it becomes at all excited or starts to play up, immediately make it stand motionless until told to walk on again.

Whenever the colt is told to stand, insist that it stands correctly every time, with both forelegs and both hindlegs, respectively, together; it should always be made to stand with its legs 'all square'. It is a particularly bad fault for it to trail one foreleg or one hindleg behind the other. Standing correctly is very important when showing a horse, whether in a ridden class, or when showing it in hand.

Standing correctly, legs together

When the colt moves forward and trots freely, and comes back to a walk or halt when told, with your assistant at its head, again tell him to relinquish his hold on the head-collar, while still walking by its head. Then repeat, walking, trotting and halting without being held, equally on both circles.

Finally it must do this by itself, without the assistant at its head.

Its reaction may be slow first when told to walk or stand from a trot. This early training on the lunge may take a short time or several weeks (or even longer), according to the colt's character, temperament and intelligence.

The colt must then be trained to wear a surcingle. First allow it to smell and examine it thoroughly before putting it on. Having put it round only fasten it sufficiently tightly to prevent it from slipping or moving its position. Only tighten it gradually after it has been worn several times. The first time it is put on, let the colt stand still until it grows used to the feel of something round it. When it accepts this, lunge it with the surcingle on.

Then fasten side-reins onto the surcingle, with the other ends attached to the head-collar. These side-reins are known as a 'dumb jockey'. The inner rein should be slightly shorter. This is to encourage it to bend its head and neck inwards in the direction in which it is circling. Readjust the relative lengths of the side-reins each time the direction of the circle is changed. Do not allow the colt to circle with its head turned outwards away from you.

Do not give titbits when lungeing, or the colt will form the bad habit of wandering into the centre expecting to be fed, especially every time it is told to stand.

The faster the colt is moving the larger the circle should be, and the longer the lungeing-rein. Keep any spare length of rein neatly coiled up in the hand which is holding it, so that it cannot become entangled with the colt's legs or your own; never allow it to trail slack on the ground. Shorten the rein as you give the order to slacken pace or stop. It is possible to get in a fearful tangle, with disastrous results, especially when schooling a young and excitable animal.

Always school on level ground in a quiet corner of the field where there are as few distractions as possible. The ideal is to lunge in a covered school, if one is fortunate enough to have the use of one.

Keep the colt moving at a steady pace, whether walking or trotting; never allow it to rush violently round so that it loses all balance and rhythm. Pull it up, using your voice, directly it tries to do so. Make it stand still and correctly until it has calmed down, and then start again.

On the other hand, do not allow it to slouch along half asleep, with its head drooping and without using its quarters, when walking. Always insist on it walking briskly round with long strides and even paces.

Insist on absolute obedience to your voice. The length of time taken to obey should gradually decrease as the colt becomes familiar with its work. At first its reactions and reflexes may be comparatively slow and one must make due allowance for that. One can almost see the colt's brain working as it thinks out the order, and finally obeys it. So if it does not react immediately when told, especially when changing from a trot to a walk, or when coming to a halt from a trot, it is not necessarily disobedience. Like human beings, some horses' minds work more slowly than others. Training will gradually quicken their response.

If one has a very excitable colt with excessively high spirits, lunge it in a confined area where it cannot break away or escape, preferably in a straw-covered yard or in a field where the going is heavy. Let it canter round and play the fool until it has exhausted itself, and then start the lungeing lesson. And keep it really hard at work; this will soon take some of the nonsense out of it. But do not attempt this in an open field or an outdoor school, unless securely closed in, or it may break away. Once it discovers its superior strength and realizes that it can break away and escape, it will continually try to do so and will be difficult to hold. Then, the only answer is to restart its schooling on the lunge, making it circle with an assistant at its head until it has learnt obedience again. It will be difficult to cure and may take a long time.

Like all youngsters, colts are full of high spirits and may indulge in a display of them and let off steam from time to time, especially when first taken out for a lesson. And one would not have it otherwise. A lifeless, dispirited colt will make a very dull ride later on, and will probably be lacking in courage. One does not want to 'break' one's colt's spirit, and one wants it to enjoy its work, so that it throws itself wholeheartedly into it. So an occasional buck at the start of the lunge-ing lesson should be regarded as quite harmless, so long as one does not lose control, and by the use of one's voice one can make the youngster settle down quickly to serious work. High spirits are not necessarily 'playing-up'. Beware of the too placid colt; you may be handling an unsuspected volcano, as resentment may be boiling up inwardly, until one day there is a sudden, and unexpected, eruption. So one must learn to distinguish between natural high spirits and deliberate naughtiness.

A colt which really plays up can become very cunning and may think out all sorts of evasions to avoid obedience. One serious one is when it moves inwards with the intention of turning its hindquarters towards one and suddenly letting out with its heels. This is potentially dangerous. Scold it severely with your voice, and push it away with the point of the whip. As it moves outwards order it sharply to walk or trot on, at the same time giving its hindquarters a really smart flick with the whiplash. Make it understand once and for all, the very first time it attempts anything like this, that you will not tolerate any such nonsense. This is one of the rare occasions when punishment is necessary. But when it obeys and has once more settled down to its work, praise it with your voice and make much of it.

Finally, when it is moving freely and obediently, it can be lunged with a bit (the one it has been accustomed to being mouthed with in the stable, but not the mouthing-bit with keys) in its mouth. At first attach this to the head-collar.

Long-reining

As the aim is to teach the colt free forward movement all the time, long-reining now plays an important part in its schooling. Like everything else in its education this new idea must be introduced gradually, step by step.

At first use the cavesson head-collar in which it is accustomed to being lunged. Attach a lungeing-rein on each side, sufficiently long to keep one well out of range of the colt's heels while walking behind it.

Besides making it move forward freely, long-reining also teaches the colt to obey signals, or aids, to stop or turn to the left or right, which are given from behind. This will introduce it to the idea of obeying aids given through the reins by a rider from on top, after it has eventually been backed and ridden, or when driven in harness.

Ask your assistant to walk by the colt's head, on the near side, and lead it by its head-collar, as in the first stage of being lunged. Your assistant moves forward when you give the order to walk on. As you do so, slacken the reins a little and lightly touch the colt's flank or hindquarters with the lungeing-whip. When you want it to stop, as you give the order to stand apply a little tension equally to both long reins, while your assistant comes to a halt. Repeat this for as many lessons as necessary until the colt understands what you want and obeys, with as little help as possible from your assistant.

To turn, say 'Turn right' (or 'left') and slightly tighten the rein on the side you want to turn, while your assistant leads the colt round in that direction. Again, repeat many times, turning right or left, until the colt understands and obeys. On achieving this, tell your assistant to walk by the colt's head without actually touching the head-collar—he should merely be there to insist on obedience if necessary when you give the orders.

Finally, make the colt turn right or left, and stand, without having anyone at its head. As always, insist on the colt standing correctly every time it halts.

When turning, besides using the appropriate rein, as you give the order lightly tap the colt's flank with the whip on the opposite side to which you want it to turn. This will introduce it to the idea, used later on, of going away from the rider's leg.

When schooling, the long schooling-whip, which can now replace the lungeing-whip, should be regarded solely as an aid; in fact merely as an extension of one's arm. The way in which one first introduces it to the colt is therefore very important. It should simply look upon it as an aid and never as something which produces pain, and therefore as something to be feared. The first time the colt is shown the whip allow it to examine it thoroughly and to smell it, to satisfy its curiosity and to reassure it that it is harmless. Then move it about slowly and gently in front of its head, at the same time speaking soothingly. Next stroke its back and sides gently with the point of the whip. Finally, when it has accepted this without any signs of fear, tap its hindquarters with the leather keeper, on the end of the whip. Repeat this daily for several days until the colt regards the schooling-whip as a perfectly normal part of the proceedings and shows no fear at all of it. It is most important that it should never be allowed to become whip-shy. Later on it can be given quite a smart tap with the whip, on the rare occasions when this may be necessary as a reminder, without it showing any signs of resentment or fear.

I have known some schooled horses to be terrified at the sight of a whip. They would not allow a rider to approach if holding one. Such fear is a sign of something being seriously wrong. It should be possible to stroke a horse's neck with one's riding-whip, when mounted or dismounted, or even to flourish it about near its head, or use it as a fly-whisk, without evoking the slightest reaction or sign of fear.

The training described so far, with lungeing and long-reining, should take the colt through its second and third years.

No attempt has been made yet to back it because its bones are still soft and immature. Backing should not be attempted until it is four years old: it can strain the spine and even cause fusion of the vertebrae through pressure of the saddle, and the rider's weight, on them. Also, if a horse is ridden when too young, especially on hard surfaces, serious damage can be done to a horse's legs, such as the formation of splints, side-bones, or sprained tendons, curb or spavins and navicular disease, and various other things which cause lameness and unsoundness, and all these can be permanent in their effects.

At this point I can hear someone say 'What nonsense! Racehorses are broken in as yearlings and raced as two-year olds.' Yes, granted. But unfortunately racing is a business with very large sums of money involved, and therefore racehorses are all too often regarded simply as money-making machines. And how many permanently break down as a result? One usually only hears of those which survive in spite of such treatment—of the successes. One does not hear of the fate of the others that do break down. If valuable, a stallion may be sent to stud, or a mare used as a brood mare. Less valuable animals, if they are lucky and have not sustained permanent injury, may be patched up, sold and re-schooled for show-jumping, while others may become riding-school hacks. I have met and ridden quite a number of ex-racehorses which have found their way into riding-schools as hacks. The rest, less fortunate (or are they?) are simply destroyed. One does not know what percentage of wastage there is each year, or the numbers of good young horses which suffer this fate.

A horse reaches maturity when it is five, and therefore should not be ridden seriously or at all hard until that age. What a public outcry there would be if a child of ten was compelled to train for, say, an attempt on the 100 yards world record. And yet in age a two-year-old horse is only equivalent in human years to a child of ten.

6 Fourth Year

The first step towards backing our four-year-old is to accustom it to the feel of something on its back and round its body, in preparation for a saddle and girth. It will be more or less prepared for the latter through wearing a surcingle when being lunged.

Backing—first step: accustom young horse to the feel of something on its back and round its body. Use an empty sack or folded blanket fastened with a surcingle

Fasten an empty sack or a folded blanket on its back with a surcingle; do not girth up the surcingle too tightly at first, but just enough to keep the blanket or sack in its correct position, where the saddle will ultimately rest, without moving. While putting this on its back let your assistant occupy its attention with a bowl of oats, or some other titbit.

If it seems at all nervous let it examine and smell the surcingle and blanket (or sack), or put them on the ground and walk away, leaving them there until it goes up and turns them over with its nose. Having thoroughly examined them and satisfied itself that they are harmless it will probably snort and walk away. That is the moment to pick them up and put them on, with your assistant standing ready at its head. Have a fairly long lead-rope attached to the head-collar, in case of trouble.

Once they are on let the colt stand still and think over this strange new indignity. If it decides to resent it look out for the probable explosion; in its efforts to rid itself of the blanket on its back it may kick, buck, rear or throw itself about; therefore the first time they are put on the colt it should be in a confined space, where it cannot escape, and on soft ground in case it falls in its struggles, or throws itself down. If it refuses to be calmed, allow it plenty of rope and let it fight until it exhausts itself and realizes that it cannot rid itself of the thing on its back, or escape from you.

When it eventually quietens down, slowly shorten the rope, speak soothingly and go up to its head with a bowl of oats. It will probably stand sweating and trembling, with a thoroughly bewildered look of abject misery and dejection. Make much of it and allow it to eat until it calms down and stands still. Then lead it slowly forward, with your assistant on the other side, also at its head in case it again tries to become violent. If it does not, lead it slowly and quietly round the enclosure until eventually it relaxes and goes round quite calmly and freely. The first lesson in carrying something on its back will have been learnt.

Repeat daily, several times a day, until it stands quietly while the blanket and surcingle are put on, meanwhile munching contentedly at a bowl of oats, and allows itself to be led about the enclosure without any fuss.

If it does not show any resentment the first time, let it stand quietly and eat from the bowl which your assistant holds out to it, and while it eats talk to it and make much of it. When it has finished, lead it slowly and quietly round with your assistant.

When the colt has accepted the feel of something on its back and a surcingle round its body, one should accustom it next to the idea of carrying a weight. Put some straw in a sack and fasten it on with the surcingle—this should not cause any trouble if one starts with only a light weight. As the colt accepts this and allows itself to be led carrying the weight, gradually increase the amount of straw each day, working up eventually to a full sack. At each stage, after leading it round several times, lunge the colt with the sack on its back.

Straw-filled sack, fastened with surcingle

When it allows itself to be led and lunged quietly with a full sack on its back, introduce it to a saddle. If it seems nervous again let it first smell and examine the saddle thoroughly. Leave it on the yard rail, or on the door of its box, for the colt to sniff at until it no longer takes any notice of it.

It is better to use a linen or felt-lined saddle for the first attempt, as one which is leather-lined feels colder on its back, especially in winter. Even a schooled, experienced horse will crouch and shrink away if a cold, leather-lined saddle is suddenly dumped on its back.

While your assistant stands at the colt's head and gives it a titbit, very quietly approach and place the saddle on its back. Lift it fairly high above its wither and slide it slowly back into its correct position. Have a nylon girth ready attached and laid across the saddle. Put the saddle on from the off (right) side, to avoid unnecessary movement in going round the colt to put the girth down. Let the girth hang down with as little movement as possible, being very careful that it does not knock against the colt's legs as it dangles. Walk round in front, not behind, bend down and pick up the girth and buckle it on loosely. Do not try to tighten it up.

If it shows no anxiety or resentment so far, let it stand and eat with the saddle on. Then, if all is still well, tighten the girth slowly, a hole at a time, until it is just tight enough to keep the saddle securely in its correct position.

There may possibly be an explosion, as when the blanket and surcingle were first put on. If so, treat it in exactly the same way; let the colt tire itself out, and then, when it has calmed down, persuade it to be led round and round the enclosure.

It is advisable to use an old saddle which does not matter much in case the colt falls or throws itself down and rolls on it, possibly breaking the tree; or a child's felt pad could be used first.

Besides leading and lungeing the colt with the weighted sack and finally the saddle on its back, also drive it every day in long reins.

There should of course be no stirrups attached at first. When the colt is thoroughly used to being led, lunged and long-reined with the saddle on, attach the stirrup leathers, leaving the irons run up. Again

Being led with saddle on, stirrups run up

lead, lunge and long-rein for as long as necessary, until it is completely accustomed to the leathers and irons.

Then repeat the same routine with the irons dangling; this will prepare the colt for the feel of a rider's legs at its sides, and for the leg aids.

Continue to lunge the colt daily, and insist on absolute obedience as regards correct stance when told to halt, smooth transitions from a walk to a trot, or *vice versa*, and from walk or trot to a halt, and so on; also insist on the colt moving briskly when walking or trotting. It must not be allowed to slop along.

If it now lunges obediently without becoming excited, it may be introduced to cantering on the lunge. Start this at first without a saddle, using the surcingle and side-reins. Start it circling at a trot and then urge it on, saying 'Canter', with your voice and a slight flick of the lungeing-whip, until it breaks into a slow canter.

Work in an enclosed space, so that it cannot break away and escape if it becomes excited and tries to start rushing round. Directly it shows any signs of becoming excited or of quickening its canter, make it halt and stand still and correctly. Talk soothingly to it until it

Saddle, no stirrups. Trotting on the lunge

Saddle, stirrups run up. Walking on the lunge

Saddle, stirrups dangling. Trotting on the lunge

has calmed down again, and then start it circling at a walk and finally another slow canter. Do this equally on both circles. It is as well at first to have your helper present, ready to go to the colt's head if necessary. He should either stand right outside the circle on which the colt is moving, well out of the way, or close behind you in the centre.

If the colt starts cantering with the wrong foreleg leading, stop it immediately, and restart. When cantering on the left circle it must lead with the left foreleg, and *vice versa*.

Similarly, stop at once and begin again if it starts cantering false (disunited), with the off-fore and near-hind instead of the off-fore and off-hind, or *vice versa* on the other circle. Also stop it if it starts changing legs behind.

All these are difficult faults to cure, and therefore must not be allowed to develop into bad habits, otherwise, later schooling will be greatly hampered (*vide* Chapter 11).

When it is cantering correctly and quietly on both circles, start lungeing it at a canter with the saddle on. At first keep the stirrup irons run up. Then finally canter it on both circles with the stirrup irons dangling. Stop immediately if it becomes upset or excited, and

Cantering on the lunge, with saddle on and stirrups run up

return to walking and trotting until it has calmed down. Then try cantering again.

Continue long-reining without a saddle, but with a snaffle bit, to teach the colt to obey the rein aids. Also give it vocal commands, such as, 'Stand', 'Walk on', 'Trot', 'Turn right' (or left).

Long rein also with the saddle on, first with the irons run up and later with them dangling, and the bit in its mouth.

7 Backing

The colt has now left its colt stage and has become a young horse, ready physically and mentally to be backed.

While your assistant holds the young horse and gives it a titbit, lean against the saddle. Do this several times with short intervals in between, putting more weight against it each time.

Backing—leaning against saddle. Assistant at horse's head

When the horse accepts this and stands still without taking any notice, put your arms over the saddle and lever yourself up until you are lying across it. Gradually increase the length of time during which you remain lying over the saddle, so long as the horse shows no signs of uneasiness.

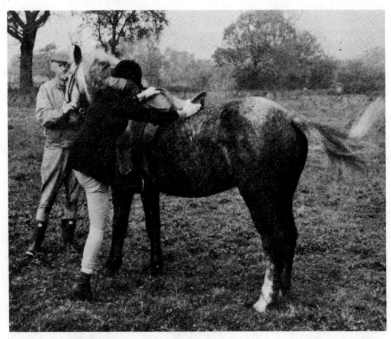

Backing—putting weight on stirrup iron

Next, put your foot in the stirrup iron and put your weight on it, raising yourself up. Let your assistant feed the horse while you do so to occupy its attention, and ask him to hold the iron on the other side to prevent the saddle from slipping round. Then dismount. Gradually increase the length of time you keep yourself raised up with your foot in the iron, with short intervals between each attempt. If it moves or appears uneasy dismount immediately.

When you can eventually stay there for about a minute without the horse fidgetting, very quietly swing your leg over and sit down, remaining absolutely motionless in the saddle. It may take several days before the horse has gained enough confidence to allow you to do this; but do not hurry it. Meanwhile your assistant should talk to the horse, make much of it and give it a titbit, while you are sitting in the saddle. Be prepared to jump off quickly at the first signs of any trouble.

Now is the time to teach the horse to stand still while being mounted and dismounted. Your assistant should stand at the horse's head, with his hands on each side just below the cheek-rings of the snaffle bit. This is the correct way to hold a horse for someone to mount. To prevent the saddle from slipping round as the rider mounts, the assistant can hold the stirrup iron with one hand. Then place your foot in the iron, raise yourself up, remain there for a few moments, and dismount. Do this a number of times, and insist on the horse standing still each time. When it does, make much of it and give it a titbit. If it does not, scold it and start again. When it has learnt to stand quietly, mount and sit still, making it stand motionless until you tell it to walk on and your assistant leads it forward. Practise this daily, every time you mount, until it has formed the habit.

In the same way, when dismounting, ask your assistant to hold the horse's head. Insist on it standing still while you take your feet out of the irons and dismount, and after you have dismounted. If it tries to fidget mount again and repeat this until it does stand quietly.

A horse which refuses to stand still while being mounted (or dismounted), is a perfect nuisance when one is riding in company, since it upsets the other horses and makes them fidget as well. It can easily cause an accident by bumping into another horse and unseating its rider, or by starting a kicking match—and make you thoroughly unpopular in the process.

It is also very useful to train a horse to stand still when the reins are thrown on its neck. It should be taught to do this when one is either mounted or dismounted. I have trained my ponies to stand still in the entrance to the stables when the reins are thrown on their neck. They will stand motionless while I run up the irons, unfasten the girth, remove the saddle and walk away to place it on the saddle horse. I can then go into the tack-room a few feet away and hang up my riding-whip on the bridle hook, while they remain in the same place. They know they must not move while the reins are lying on their neck. If they do move I have only to say, 'Now, stand'. Then, when they are told to, they will follow me into the stall without being led. They will also stand for me outside a shop if I throw the reins on their neck and say 'Stand'. This is extremely useful on many occasions.

The time to start this training is after the horse has been backed, when it is being taught to stand while being mounted or dismounted. Once having learnt this, teaching the horse to stand when the reins are thrown on its neck can follow quite naturally as the next step in its training. Even older horses can be trained given time and patience.

Long-reining is still continued, the aim being to teach the horse to obey signals given by the reins, and to flex his jaw, accepting the bit and bridling to it.

Continue to lunge for about twenty minutes before the start of each lesson. This gives the horse a chance to let off steam and get rid of some of its high spirits before settling down to serious work. It also may save you a fall should it start playing up or bucking when you have mounted.

A horse dislikes it when its rider comes off; it is also bad for it psychologically, as once it discovers that it can get rid of its rider it may form the habit of deliberately trying to unseat him. One then has the makings of a potential bucking broncho. Furthermore if the rider lets go of the reins as he falls and the horse discovers that it can escape and gain its freedom, it may form the habit of galloping off and re-fusing to be caught again.

Also, your assistant should lunge the horse daily while you ride it. You can then make it canter on the lunge and ensure that it leads with the correct leg and does not canter false or disunited; the inside leg is the correct one to lead with on whichever circle it is being lunged. Lunge it equally on both circles, making it lead on each with its in-side leg. If it does not, bring it back to a trot and start again.

While being lunged, teach it to understand the leg aids to halt, walk on, trot and turn, and to neck-rein, to the right or left.

When teaching the aids make them very clear and definite, even though the ultimate aim is to school your horse to respond to the lightest possible leg or rein pressure. The aids then become almost invisible to the onlooker and it appears as if some sort of telepathy exists between horse and rider.

Next do the same without halting at each corner before turning to left or right. Ride it right into and round at each corner, pushing its hindquarters round as it turns, first walking, and then trotting in both directions through the corners. Do a rising trot along the sides and ends of the school and a sitting trot round the corners.

Practise, walking and trotting, using diagonal aids, and when the horse has mastered these, teach it to respond in the same way to lateral aids.

It is a sign of bad, 'sloppy' riding to allow a horse to cut its corners while it is being schooled. Naturally, when practising at a canter, at a more advanced stage, the horse will be unable to go right into the corners owing to the faster pace. But it should be ridden as nearly as possible into them, 'going large' as it is called.

At first canter round the sides and ends of the school and bring it back to a sitting, collected, trot as it corners. This will also prevent it from becoming excited and out of control, as a young horse tends to become when being cantered round the school. If it does become excited, bring it back to a halt, standing correctly, and then again start it at a canter.

While making the young horse's mouth the first bit should be a straight-barred, fairly thick rubber or vulcanite snaffle.

First bit—rubber snaffle. EQUIPMENT KINDLY SUPPLIED BY MOSS BROS.

If the youngster is excitable and inclined to throw its head about, or hold it too high, it may be necessary to introduce it to a standing martingale, used just tight enough to prevent it from throwing its head up above the normal height. It should not impair ordinary free movement of the horse's head. Do not have the martingale too tight to try and force the horse's head down; rather try to persuade it to hold it in the correct position by using your seat and hands. An excitable young horse which throws its head up is sometimes inclined to try to take hold of the bit and bolt.

If a rubber or vulcanite straight bit is not strong enough to enable you to hold or control it, try an egg-butt jointed snaffle, or, if necessary, a plain jointed (or 'broken') snaffle with a fairly thick mouthpiece. But use the mildest bit possible which will enable you to control it. When a horse is difficult to control the usual tendency is to use a still stronger bit, which makes matters worse as the horse fights against the bit in its endeavours to fight against the increased pain which is being inflicted on its mouth. This is simply a vicious circle and ultimately ends in making the horse hard-mouthed.

It is most important to keep the horse balanced and 'soft' on both sides of its mouth. If always lunged on the same circle, or otherwise worked in only one direction, its neck muscles become more developed on one side than the other. Hence the importance of doing everything equally, lungeing, turning, and so on, to the right and to the left, so that the muscles develop on both sides.

In the same way, always ride equally on both diagonals when trotting, (i.e., when doing a rising trot). This may seem elementary, obvious common-sense, but I have had ponies and horses to school which had been worked only in one direction; they were completely one-sided and unresponsive when asked to turn or bend in the opposite direction. Again, when a horse is always trotted on the same diagonal it feels most uncomfortable and one-sided when trotted on the other, opposite diagonal. It should feel equally balanced, even and comfortable when ridden on either diagonal. In fact it should be impossible to tell on which diagonal it is being ridden. So work equally to left and to right when lungeing, long-reining and riding. Everything done on the left rein should immediately be done on the right rein, and *vice versa*.

The horse has so far been backed and has learnt the leg and rein aids for the ordinary walk, trot and canter, ridden both on and off the lunge-rein. It can now be taught to go 'on the bit'.

The meaning of this has already been discussed. Up to now it has been asked to relax its jaw and move with only a very light rein contact with the bit. It must now learn not only to relax its jaw, but also to hold the bit softly in its mouth with a light rein contact, and to keep it there while being asked to move at all paces and in any direction. Until it can and will do so, any more advanced work is impossible.

If it resists, use the reins with the same movement of the hand and fingers as before (likened to that of squeezing a sponge) to make it relax its jaw and hold the bit.

To trot correctly the horse must use its hindlegs actively and swing its back; it cannot circle correctly or corner smoothly unless it can do this. When circling, its inside legs must take shorter strides than its outside legs.

If the horse is stiff and does not use its back, its hocks cannot bend enough, and it cannot bring them sufficiently under it, to make its hindlegs follow exactly in the imprints of its forelegs. So the hindlegs are thrown outwards and move in a larger circle than the forelegs.

Teaching it to perform half-halts will supple it lengthwise. Use the the same aids as when asking it to change from a trot to a walk, but make it trot again just before it actually starts walking.

A halt means the way that the horse is stopped at the end of a movement. It is achieved by displacing its weight onto its quarters. This is done by sitting deep into the saddle and closing the legs, while resisting with the hands. This makes the horse stop instantly, while its legs remain ready to continue impulsion.

To perform a half-halt the rider's hands act to prepare the horse either for a halt or for a transition from a quicker to a slower pace. By shifting more of its weight onto its quarters it makes it easier for the horse to engage its hindlegs and maintain its balance on its haunches.

Having taught it to go on the bit, it can then learn the variations of the three natural paces, walk, trot and canter.

When doing a collected walk make the horse walk determinedly forward, with its neck raised and arched and its head nearly vertical. The rider keeps a light contact with its mouth through the reins. Its hindlegs move with vigorous hock action at a steady march pace and even steps. These are slightly shorter in the collected walk than in the ordinary walk, with each step covering slightly less ground. The hind-feet touch the ground slightly behind the imprints made by the fore-feet. This ensures that the cadence (or rhythm) of the collected walk does not become hurried and irregular, or uneven. As all the joints bend more, each step is higher than in the ordinary walk.

Collected walk on lunge

Collected walk off lunge

When learning an extended walk the horse must cover as much ground as possible without hurrying. Its steps must be even and regular. Its head is carried in front of the vertical, with both head and neck outstretched. The rider's hands must maintain contact with the bit. In contrast to the collected walk, in an extended walk the hindfeet come to the ground in front of the imprints made by the forefeet.

The free walk on a long rein rewards the horse after working, by allowing it complete freedom to stretch out its head and neck.

A collected trot is slower than the ordinary trot; the horse takes shorter steps. Its head is raised allowing its shoulders to move freely. Its hocks are well under and it moves energetically. The rider sits when doing a collected trot.

Riding on a long rein after work. Horse stretching out head and relaxing neck muscles. 'Rewarding' the horse

Ordinary trot on the lunge

In an extended trot the horse lengthens its stride to cover as much ground as possible. It also stretches out its neck while a light rein contact is kept on it, and its quarters move with impulsion, which makes it use its shoulders. Thus it covers more ground at each step without having a higher action. The extended trot is performed as a rising trot.

When performing a collected canter the horse's quarters are very active, while its shoulders are supple and free. Impulsion is maintained with greater movement.

In an extended canter the horse remains calm, and lengthens its stride without increasing its pace. It is light on the bit. Its neck is extended so that the tip of its nose is pointing more or less forward.

8 Importance of Short Lessons

It is important to keep the lessons short to prevent a young horse from becoming bored or over-tired. Also, as already stressed (Chapter 5), the young horse's muscles and bones are still not yet fully developed, and therefore must not be subjected to undue strain. So forty to forty-five minutes is quite long enough for a schooling if the horse is kept alert and working hard the whole time. Two short schooling periods, one in the morning and one in the afternoon, are far more valuable than a single long one, with the risk of boredom and physical over-strain.

If it becomes over-tired there is the risk of injury to its muscles and bones, particularly its legs and vertebrae. If forced to work when over-tired it may become soured, sullen and obstinate, and even end by refusing, and inventing all sorts of evasions. The more it is forced when this stage is reached, the more obstinate, stubborn and unwilling to co-operate it becomes.

A horse should enjoy its work, and at all costs one wants to preserve its natural spontaneity and gaiety. One does not want to break its spirit and natural courage.

When one feels that it is becoming physically tired, and/or bored, either take it for a quiet hack after its schooling, to keep it interested and allow it to relax mentally and physically, or, ride it round the field on a long rein; this rewards it by allowing it to stretch out its head and neck and relax its jaw. During its schooling its head and neck muscles have been kept in a constrained and more or less un-natural position, and are probably aching. How often when one rides a horse on a long rein after schooling, will one see it gratefully stretch out its neck, lower its head and reach for its bit?

An essential part of a young horse's training will be to accustom it to a variety of sights and sounds—the more varied the better. If one lives on a farm, or there is one near, let it see stationary and moving tractors and lorries; also cattle and sheep. The more strange objects it encounters daily, the better.

If it shows fear or suspicion of something, persuade it to go up to the object; lead it if necessary. After it has thoroughly examined and smelt it, it will lose all interest and fear. Then ride it past the object several times until it is completely unconcerned.

If you have a dog, let the horse become thoroughly accustomed to it gambolling about and barking. It will meet many irresponsible dogs during its life, so the sooner it becomes used to them, the better. You must train your dog not to go near your horse's heels, or to snap at them. Even the most placid horse will object to being nipped, and a dog which has been kicked on the head and had its skull split open is not a pleasant sight. Nor can one blame the horse.

It is essential for a horse to be absolutely traffic-proof, especially these days. At first ride it in quiet country lanes so that it becomes indifferent to the occasional passing car. Gradually accustom it to stand near a car while it is being started, and then while it is being revved up.

Motor-cycles can be a serious danger on the roads to a horse which is at all 'nervy' or inclined to be traffic-shy. Some motor-cyclists are considerate and slow up, shutting off their engines, as they pass, but some younger members of the fraternity think it funny to rev up just as they come up from behind, and then to pass as close as they can. If they succeed in frightening the horse, that makes their day. If they only knew the danger to their own skins they would think twice before doing it; the horse has only to shy and swing its hindquarters outwards into them, to send them flying. And at the speed at which they are moving it would inevitably put them in hospital for many weeks, or even send them rather suddenly to a premature grave. If you meet one of these motor-cyclists, keep a firm hold on both reins and turn your horse's head outwards, so that if it shies, it will swing its hindquarters inwards towards the hedge.

Introduce the young horse to lorries as soon as possible; take the earliest opportunity to ride it up to a stationary lorry and let it examine and smell it thoroughly until 'familiarity breeds contempt'. If it is suspicious and refuses to approach the lorry, dismount and lead the horse up to it rather than increase its fear by forcing it. Once it has satisfied itself that this monster has no evil intentions towards it, mount, and then ride up and down several times past the lorry, until the horse passes it without any hesitation. If it is possible, ride a little distance away and then ask the driver to start the engine. If it panics, dismount and let the horse stand as near to the lorry as you can persuade it; then lead it past the lorry several times. Repeat this until it becomes accustomed to it. Then mount and ride past it several times. Once the horse has satisfied itself that it has nothing to fear, you should have no further trouble.

Personally I have found that the majority of lorry-drivers are extremely considerate. They invariably slow up when approaching or overtaking, and I have even known an approaching driver to stop and switch off his engine while we passed. But if you meet one that does not slow up (there are a few about), do not tense or in any way let your horse feel that you expect any trouble. If you tense it makes your horse think that you are afraid, and that makes it suspect that there is danger. Merely be alert, with reins fairly short in both hands, without tightening them, and your knees close to the saddle, ready to grip hard if necessary. Turn your horse's head outwards and press your right leg against its flank behind the girth, to prevent it from swinging its hindquarters round outwards, should it suddenly panic and shy.

All motor traffic by law is supposed to give way to anyone leading, riding or driving a horse, and to slow up, especially if signalled to do so. But not all motorists, apparently, know the Highway Code; the weekend driver and holiday-maker are the worst offenders, particularly the young blood with his girl friend in a fast, noisy sports car, who wants to show off.

It is an excellent thing to be accompanied by a staid old bridlewise horse, to act as 'schoolmaster' when taking a youngster out on the road for the first few times. Ride the young horse alongside, on the inside next to the grass verge or kerb. Having the company of another horse often seems to inspire confidence in a 'nervy' horse. A horse that is inclined to shy at traffic when alone will often pass the biggest and noisiest vehicle quite unconcernedly when with another horse, especially if the latter is completely traffic-proof.

When the young horse's training in traffic is well advanced, find a busy road, preferably with a wide grass verge, and take every opportunity to ride along it, especially at weekends. Be accompanied at first by the 'schoolmaster'.

Police horses have to become completely immune to every conceivable kind of object and noise; part of their training consists of having rattles swung under their noses, umbrellas opened suddenly just in front of them, pistols fired and fireworks exploded both in front of and behind them, motor-cycles or cars back-firing, and so on, until they become completely unperturbed.

My own mare will stand quite unconcerned on top of a railway bridge, while a heavy goods train with a steam locomotive passes directly underneath. And she treats tractors, bulldozers and even the biggest vehicles on the road with complete indifference, and utter contempt. This is simply the result of constant gradual training over the years that I have ridden her. Yet she has been known to shy at and refuse to pass a suspicious-looking log in a wood, when it was growing dusk.

9 Introduction to Jumping

When it is rising five the youngster will be ready for its first jumping lessons. Jumping comes naturally to most horses and the majority of young ones love it—until they are put off by receiving a bad jab in the mouth.

One pony I have jumps electric fences with the utmost contempt: indeed it is impossible to keep him in any one particular paddock. He even jumped out of the paddock clearing well over four feet six inches, until I was compelled to raise the fence. Yet he is normally one of the laziest ponies I have ever met, especially to lead.

One of the best ways to start schooling a young horse to jump is to use its natural love for it, and to make it jump free in a 'Weedon' jumping-lane. This took its name originally from the Army Equitation School at Weedon (now no longer in existence) where this method of training young horses to jump was used. It is a straight, narrow lane, fenced in on both sides so that the horse cannot get out. Low fences are placed along it at intervals. The youngster enters at one end and has to jump the obstacles in order to get out at the other end. Most horses and ponies thoroughly enjoy this, especially if they are rewarded with a titbit at the other end.

Schooling in a jumping-lane teaches young horses to balance themselves and to jump freely. It can also be used for older horses to renew their interest when they have grown stale, or become bored, through being jumped too much; or for restoring their confidence and nerve when they have been put off jumping by a bad jab in the mouth, or a bad fall.

An unridden horse seldom refuses or makes a mistake and very rarely, if ever, falls. As witness riderless horses, which, having dislodged their jockey in a race, continue to jump every fence, frequently right up with the leaders.

It is a wise plan to let a good jumper lead and act as schoolmaster when first introducing a young horse to the jumping-lane.

Another way of teaching a horse to jump freely is to place low obstacles around the circumference of a circle and to make it jump them on the lungeing-rein. Do this in an enclosed space so that the horse cannot run out, or pull away and escape if it becomes excited.

Once the horse is jumping freely by itself over a variety of small obstacles (the more varied the better), the next step is teaching it to jump when ridden. Having a rider on its back at first completely upsets its natural balance, so that it has to readjust itself.

Place six or seven *cavalletti* in a row, some ten to twelve feet apart. They should be solidly built so that they will not move easily, and will make the horse respect them and lift up its feet. In fact all jumps should be fairly solid (or at any rate should look solid). Flimsy jumps which fall down at the slightest touch are worse than useless for schooling. As soon as the horse discovers that they fall when it raps them, it treats them with contempt and becomes careless about lifting its feet and legs. Completely solid, immovable jumps, however, are dangerous as they can give a horse a bad fall, which will put it off jumping for a long time, perhaps permanently. If a horse once really loses its nerve and confidence it takes a long time to regain it.

Walking over 'cavalletti'

At first make it step over the *cavalletti* at a walk. Insist on it picking up its feet and clearing the *cavalletti* without touching them. Practise this daily for short periods, but do not allow the horse to become bored with it. The *cavalletti* should be about ten inches high for the first exercise. Practise at an ordinary walk, and then at a collected and an extended walk.

Trotting over 'cavalletti'

When it can walk over the *cavalletti* without touching them, turn them over so that they are about fifteen inches high and make it trot over them. Do this at a sitting and a rising trot, and again insist on the horse picking up its feet and clearing them without touching. Make it trot over in both directions. If it grows excited bring it back to a walk and start again. Practise daily for short periods, but avoid boredom. Practise also at a collected and an extended trot, as well as an ordinary trot.

The final stage in this elementary work with *cavalletti* is to turn them over to a height of nineteen inches and make the horse canter over them, at a slow, collected canter, again clearing them without touching. Work in both directions for short periods every day; only continue as long as the horse is interested. Also practise at an ordinary and extended canter. Assume the normal jumping position, weight on knees, with hands forward and low, as the horse canters over. Shorten the stirrup leathers a couple of holes. Do not allow the horse to become excited; if it does, bring it to a halt and start again, or go back first to trotting over before resuming schooling at a canter.

As the ridden horse has to learn to rebalance itself when jumping, the rider's position is important. That is the reason for the modern forward seat, which was first expounded by Caprilli. It places the rider so that his centre of gravity coincides with that of the horse. His weight also comes on the strongest part of the horse, behind

Modern jumping-seat—correct position of rider

the wither, on the deepest part, between it and the girth-groove.

Two things are necessary to enable a horse to jump freely: (1) as the impulsion comes from its hindquarters, which should therefore bring its haunches well underneath and make it jump off its hocks, the rider's weight should be off its weakest part, its loins. At its loin, between the end of its false ribs and the hip bone there are only the vertebrae (backbone or spine); (2) a horse balances itself with its head and neck when cantering, galloping or jumping. The faster the pace the more it stretches them out; the same applies to it when jumping. It must be free to stretch out its head and neck.

Therefore with the modern jumping-seat the rider sits well forward, taking his weight on his knees. To allow the horse the necessary freedom to stretch out its head and neck, the rider drops his hands forward and low as he feels the horse take off. On landing he reassumes his position in order to take his weight off the horse's forehand, because for a fraction of a second one foreleg has to take the whole weight of the horse. The impact is tremendous, especially on a hard surface. This is the most dangerous moment, the landing, when the horse is most likely to become unbalanced and peck or fall.

Vary the distance between the *cavalletti* when practising at all three paces, so that the horse keeps alert and learns to judge distances accurately, and adapts its steps accordingly. Otherwise, if the *cavalletti* are always the same distance apart it becomes so familiar with them that it grows careless.

For a single canter stride place the *cavalletti* about ten feet apart. Then make it canter over them when they are twelve feet and then twenty feet—two canter strides—apart.

The distances apart will naturally vary with the size of the horse and the length of its natural stride at a walk, trot and canter. It will also vary with a collected and extended movement at all three paces. For a pony the *cavalletti* may be closer together, e.g., eighteen feet apart for an ordinary double-canter stride, according to its size.

The height and width of the jumps are not what matter in schooling; a variety of jumps, such as a brushwood, small gate or wall, single, double or triple jump, and so on, is more important. Old railway sleepers make good jumps and have the advantage of being solid and heavy.

When a horse has completed its preliminary *cavalletti* training— which is important and should not be hurried—make it trot over low jumps. These can be made with *cavalletti* arranged in different ways; two placed close together can form a spread, the width of which can gradually be increased. One on top of two others can make a 'hog's-back', or they can form a double or eventually a triple, giving increased height and spread to make the horse extend and use itself.

Never over-face a young horse, and limit the height to about two feet six inches and the width to about five feet for quite a long time.

If jumping in a straight line excites it, arrange the jumps round a large circle, varying the distance between each, or jump them in some irregular order. A horse usually jumps more freely when facing in the direction of the entrance, probably because it thinks that it is re-turning to its stable; therefore insist on it also jumping when it is going away from the gate.

It is essential to have a firm, independent seat when schooling a youngster over jumps, as one bad jab in the mouth can completely put it off jumping. It is a good plan to use a neck-strap to hold onto when jumping so that one cannot inadvertently pull the horse's mouth. Jumping without reins is also very good for one's seat.

It is important to have the jumping-school in some quiet spot, free from distractions. Again an indoor school is invaluable, if one can have the use of one, as one can shut the doors and ensure peace and quiet, and it enables one to continue schooling when the weather is too bad to jump outdoors.

Keep the jumping lessons short to prevent overtiring or boring the young horse. And do not make it sick of jumping by riding it repeatedly over the same jump. If it appears to be growing stale discontinue the jumping sessions for a few days and substitute some other form of schooling. Always end the lesson with a good jump. Never allow the horse to end with an unsuccessful jump or a refusal, as this has a bad psychological effect and it will probably start the next lesson by refusing. Do not allow it to form the habit of refusing; if necessary push it through the jump rather than let it stop or run out.

If a normally keen and willing jumper suddenly starts consistently refusing, see if there is any cause: sore shins, a sore mouth or pain from the bit, or an uncomfortable saddle or bridle, and so on. Make certain that the saddle is not pressing down on the horse's spine as it jumps. If it is, put a sheepskin or fairly thick 'foam' numnah, or a soft felt one, on under the saddle.

Again our staid old 'schoolmaster' friend, a known and consistently willing jumper, can be used to give a lead. Only, never follow too close behind another horse over a jump. If the leading horse does happen to peck or fall as it lands the one following can easily jump on top of it and have a bad accident.

If the horse tries to run out put wings on each side of the jump, or ask someone to stand at the side on which it runs out. Only be careful that they do not get knocked over if the horse suddenly decides to swerve. Use your opposite rein, and your leg very strongly on the side on which it attempts to run out.

Go for a short quiet hack after the jumping session to keep the horse interested, and to take its mind off jumping.

Never allow a horse to form the habit of trying to rush its fences. If it does, pull it up and make it do a rein-back to calm and steady it before trying again. Collect and steady it before each jump. Vary the pace; sometimes trot instead of cantering over. The old rule is, 'slow over timber and fast over water'. Some horses dislike jumping water, so if possible, it is advisable to include a water jump in the school.

When out hacking (not after a jumping lesson), put the horse over small obstacles such as narrow ditches, fallen logs, bales of straw or hay, or the odd small fence. Do not jump hedges. There may be wire concealed in them, and if you happen to break through and damage them you will be very unpopular with the owner, and liable to be prosecuted and made to pay damages.

10 Getting a Horse Fit

There is no better way of getting a horse fit and of developing its muscles than by giving it plenty of walking or trotting exercise. A large part of the training of racehorses consists of walking, especially up and down hills. Hunters brought up from grass at the end of summer are given an increasing amount of walking exercise, to get rid of their grass bellies and to harden them up before cub-hunting begins. Also, give the young horse some slow cantering over a short distance, and a short, sharp canter about once a week to open its lungs and clear its windpipe. Exercise it for about one-and-a-half hours in the morning and the same again in the afternoon.

A certain amount of road-walking will help to harden its feet, but avoid trotting on a hard road, or it may cause navicular, splints, or other leg troubles. But do not let a young horse do much galloping, especially on soft, heavy going; besides the risk to its legs there is the danger of breaking its wind.

If the youngster has been regularly lunged, schooled and jumped up to now it should already be pretty fit. But when exercising, start with less and gradually increase the time and distance as it becomes fit and its muscles develop.

Increase the corn ration with the work—the horse's size and temperament should govern the amount actually given. A rather slow, lethargic horse which needs sharpening up can safely be given more than an excitable one which 'hots up' easily. Ponies carrying children should not be given corn unless they are doing very hard work, and then only a small ration. Again the amount depends upon the pony's temperament and its rider's ability to handle it.

Our young horse should now be ready to be introduced to hunting. For the first few times let it be accompanied by its steady old school-master friend, who is already an experienced hunter and therefore unlikely to become excited.

Take it to its first Meet simply to introduce it to hounds and to accustom it to the sight and sound of a large number of other horses. As their presence will almost certainly excite it, keep it well away from other horses, on the outskirts of the crowd.

When it first sees hounds make it stand still, and if they come up keep its head turned towards them, in case a too venturesome hound comes near its heels and it kicks out at it. Kicking a hound is the un-forgivable sin in the hunting field.

Even a normally placid horse will become excited by the atmosphere of a Meet. And an excited horse which does not usually kick is liable to let out with its heels, which is an added reason for keeping well away from other riders. Your horse may not kick, but you also do not want to risk having it kicked.

When hounds move off, move off as well, in the opposite direction, and go for a quiet hack to allow your youngster to calm down again.

At the next Meet take it to the first covert and teach it, again well away from other horses, to stand still while the hounds draw. When they find, go for a hack.

After one or two more Meets let the young horse follow, if it is a slow hunt, for a few fields. If there are a few small hedges or fences let it jump them, but directly it starts to become excited pull up and go for a hack to calm down.

A little quiet hunting often does wonders in 'settling' a young, excitable horse. But do not over-gallop or over-jump a young horse in its first season's hunting. If you value it and want it to last, spare a thought for its legs and wind! Only stay out for a short time at the beginning, say half-an-hour, gradually increasing it to an hour or an hour and a half. A couple of hours at most is ample towards the end of its first season.

According to the horse's temperament it may be necessary to use a stronger bit than normal for hunting. If usually ridden in a straight-barred snaffle, try a jointed snaffle. If it becomes excited and pulls in a snaffle, try using a Pelham or a Kimblewick, but use the mildest bit which will enable you to stop and hold it, in order to keep its mouth soft. If it throws its head about a standing martingale may be necessary.

The majority of horses love hunting and seem to know when they are going out, even in the stable. Watch an old hunter in its paddock if the hunt passes near, how it throws up its head and gallops round the field in wild excitement when it hears hounds giving tongue, or the sound of the horn. It will remain excited for hours afterwards, and woe betide you if you want to catch and ride it.

11 Dressage

The young horse is now ready to start learning elementary dressage. Until fairly recently 'dressage' seems to have been a much misunderstood word. Many hunting people and ordinary riders have scorned it, while to its enthusiasts and fanatics it has become the be-all and end-all of their riding.

But surely there is a middle course?

Perhaps the best definition of ordinary elementary dressage is the French word '*agréeable*': to make a horse balanced, obedient and light on the bit; to make it in fact, more 'agreeable'—a better ride. That would seem to be its purpose for the ordinary rider. For this reason dressage should form an important part of any horse's training.

One may wish the young horse to specialize—go in for show-jumping, one- or three-day events, or dressage competitions; or one may want it to become a show hack if its conformation is good enough.

Dressage training will undoubtedly help its performance in show-jumping, while in one- or three-day events it forms an essential part of the competition. And a course of dressage will also improve it as a show hack.

Before beginning the horse's elementary dressage schooling, accustom it to a jointed or an egg-butt snaffle for daily use. If it tends to poke its nose out, try it in a Pelham, in order to bring its nose down and its head more into its chest, by using the lower rein to act like a curb bit. But be very careful not to ride continually on the lower curb rein, or its mouth will become numb; ride on the snaffle rein.

If it tends to hold its head too high, an egg-butt or a jointed snaffle bit will help to lower it. The egg-butt is the slightly milder of the two as there is less risk of pinching the corners of its lips.

For elementary dressage it can be ridden in a single, snaffle bridle, but for more advanced work, or if the horse is going to be shown, then it will have to be accustomed to wearing a double bridle, and be schooled in it. But for hacking, jumping and hunting, it should always be ridden in the snaffle bridle.

There are numerous types of curb bits, but the most generally used are the Weymouth or the Ward Union. The Weymouth was devised by Lord Weymouth in the eighteenth century, while the Ward Union

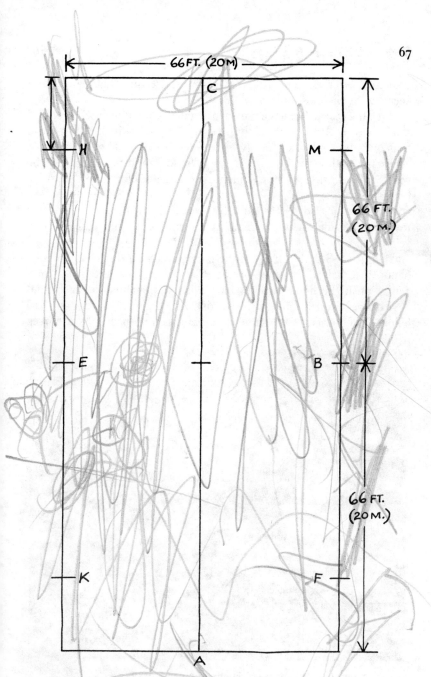

Plan of dressage arena (as used for Pony Club 'V' test)

is named after the Hunt of that name in Ireland. The Weymouth seems to be the most popular today.

But all experts have their own particular choice of bits. It is said that 'there is a key to every horse's mouth', but this does not mean that one should be constantly experimenting and changing the bit, especially with a young horse's newly 'made' mouth. Ultimately the real 'key' is a firm and independent seat, and therefore light, sensitive hands.

If the young horse has already been taught to back in its early training as a foal, it is a comparatively simple matter to teach it to rein back.

FIRST STAGE   Stand in front of the horse, and hold the bridle in both hands just below the cheek-rings. Say 'back', and the same time gently push the horse straight back with your hands on the bridle.

If it does not respond, or if it resists, tread gently on its hoof just below the coronet, at the same time again saying 'back'. As it moves

Teaching horse to rein back—first stage: rider at its head

its leg back, tread on the other hoof and again say 'back'. Be satisfied at first with even a couple of steps straight back. Stop immediately if it begins to turn its hindquarters out sideways. Then say 'walk', at the same time leading it forward two or three steps towards you.

Always insist on it moving forwards or backwards in an absolutely straight line with even steps, and on it standing correctly and balanced with its legs together when it stops.

As an alternative to treading on its hoof, lightly tap the leg which you want it to move back with the schooling-whip just above its fet-lock joint, again saying 'back' as you do so.

When the horse understands and begins mentally to associate the word 'back' with walking backwards, it will gradually begin to re-spond, until eventually it will move forwards at the word 'walk' and backwards when told to 'back'. When it does, vary the number of steps both forwards and backwards, so that it does not merely become an automatic reaction.

Teaching horse to rein back—second stage: rider mounted, assistant at horse's head. Note the poles—to keep the horse straight

SECOND STAGE   Mount and ask an assistant to stand at the horse's head, as you did in the first stage. When you give the order to walk forward, together with the correct leg and rein aids to make it walk, your assistant should gently lead the horse forward the number of steps you want, until you give the order to 'stand' (or 'whoa').

As you give the order 'back', press the horse with your knees as if you wanted it to walk forward, but resist with your hands so that it comes up against the bit when it tries to move forward. Being unable to go forward, it should step back. As you give the order and the aids, your assistant gently pushes the horse back, treading on each hoof in turn, or lightly tapping its legs with the schooling-whip if it resists or does not respond.

Never pull it back with your hands or the horse will try to throw up its head, turn its head sideways, or move its hindquarters sideways— any evasion in fact to escape from the pain inflicted through having the bit forced back against the corners of its lips. And it may make a young horse rear up if it is pulled back by the reins.

Again, be satisfied at first with only two or three steps straight back when it responds. Keep it balanced and moving back straight and evenly with your hands and legs; if it tries to swing its hindquarters out sideways, use your leg more strongly behind the girth on the side towards which it is trying to turn, to push its hindquarters in again. At the same time reinforce your leg with the rein on the opposite side. Shift your weight slightly back towards the cantle without moving the position of your seat in the saddle.

The object of this second stage is to teach the horse to understand and obey the words 'walk', 'stand' and 'back', and to associate them with their corresponding aids given when mounted.

As you give a leg aid use your voice at the same time so that the horse learns to recognize the appropriate word of command. Eventually it will obey leg and rein without any verbal order. When used for teaching beginners, riding-school horses become so accustomed to hearing the orders given by the instructor that they obey automatically without waiting for their riders to give the aids, especially when following each other round in the *manège* or a covered school.

When schooling, reward obedience instantly by sitting still and giving the horse a pat on the neck. If it does not immediately respond repeat the word of command and the leg aid.

Concentrate on teaching only one aid at a time until the horse understands and obeys it, even if this takes several lessons; otherwise you will only confuse it. Again, do not expect an immediate reaction at first, but allow enough time to elapse for the horse to think it out. Its reflex action will quicken with practice.

When teaching it to halt, say 'Stand', close your legs on the saddle and put your weight slightly back onto the horse's loins, without moving your seat back in the saddle.

To teach it to move forward, say 'Walk on', while pressing your knees on the saddle and using your back as an aid to drive your seat forwards and downwards onto the saddle. If the horse does not respond to knee pressure only, repeat the word of command, and as you press your knees against the saddle squeeze with the calves of your legs slightly behind the girth. If this brings no response, use your heels fairly sharply behind the girth, with more knee and calf pressure, while again giving the order, 'Walk on'. Carry a fairly long schooling-whip and tap the horse lightly on the flanks, behind the saddle, if it does not respond and obey.

Too much kicking against its sides can easily make a horse, especially a young one, unresponsive and 'dead on the leg'; it is better to use the whip lightly as an added aid. Sometimes with a very lazy, lethargic horse even quite a sharp cut with the whip may be necessary to wake it up and make it pay attention to its work.

When teaching it to turn left or right, look, and lean your body slightly in the direction in which you want the horse to turn; at the same time say 'Right' or 'Turn right' (or left), using your outside leg behind the girth and your inside leg at the girth. Teach the horse to go away from your leg. Again, reinforce your leg aid with the whip, used very lightly, until the horse understands what you want and obeys the leg aid.

When it has learnt to obey the leg aids teach it in the *manège* to obey the rein aids; in other words the aids given through the bit via the reins, by your hands. The horse has to learn to accept the bit and hold it lightly in its mouth, without any evasions such as getting its tongue over the bit (i.e., above the bar of the bit), rolling its tongue up behind the bar (tongue drawn back towards its throat), leaning on the bit so that it feels dead and heavy on the rider's hands, dropping the bit by bringing its mouth in towards its chest (getting behind the bit), or raising its head with a stiff poll, and taking the bit's pressure on its lips instead of on the bars of its mouth (getting above the bit). It must also learn to flex or 'give' with its jaw (i.e., relax it), in response to tension on one or both reins, according to the aid being given.

When the horse is 'on the bit', it does not offer any resistance to the rider and there is light contact with its mouth through the reins. Its head then keeps steadily in the correct position with its neck more or less raised or stretched out according to whether the rider is asking for a collected or an extended action. And its hocks are correctly used and placed.

So long as it either holds the bit passively in its mouth, or resists by setting its jaw, or by taking hold of the bit, it is impossible to give aids through the reins or to make it obey.

Directly it reacts and responds to the tension of the rein or reins by flexing its jaw, reward it by relaxing the pressure on the bit until you want to give another aid. Continuous pulling on the reins will only make the horse resist and pull in return; it will numb the bars of the mouth on which the bit rests, eventually deadening it and giving the horse a hard mouth. Heavy hands which do not 'give and take', will ruin any horse's mouth, especially a young one. That is why anyone who undertakes the schooling of a young horse must have a firm and completely independent seat, so that the rider's hands are concerned only with sending messages to the horse through its mouth, via the bit.

I always try to impress on pupils that the reins are simply like 'telegraph wires' for the purpose of sending messages. They are *not* a convenient means of 'strap-hanging' to keep oneself in the saddle. In fact my pupils are not allowed to touch the reins until they have acquired an absolutely independent seat, and have learnt to use their legs correctly, at a walk, trot and canter while being led or lunged.

This is also another important reason why only one person should ride and school a young horse until its mouth has been 'made', and it has learnt to accept the bit, and bridle, to flex its jaw and respond to the rein aids. As no two people ride exactly alike, two different people riding a young horse in process of being schooled will only muddle and confuse it in obeying both rein and leg aids.

When teaching the rein aids use your voice while giving the aid, so that the horse learns to obey the appropriate verbal order.

Teach the horse first to obey the rein aids to halt, walk on, trot and turn; use your hands and wrists with an action resembling that of squeezing a sponge. Always use the least amount of tension on the reins which will produce the desired result. Never pull the horse's head with the rein or reins, especially when turning, and never jerk or tug at the reins. When turning push the horse's hindquarters round with the appropriate leg aid or aids, so that it turns on its own centre of gravity.

If the horse does not obey, relax the tension and then give the aid again. One too often sees a rider become impatient and jab the horse's mouth with the rein when it does not obey. This is absolutely wrong. Besides ruining a young horse's mouth and deadening it, causing pain will only make it fear the bit. Not only will it refuse to flex and not be on the bit, but it will throw up its head and try every sort of evasion, even to napping, rearing or bolting if upset sufficiently, in order to escape the pain in its mouth which it is anticipating.

All tension on the rein or reins should be applied smoothly and should be relaxed as soon as the horse flexes and obeys. Anyone who is impatient or who cannot control their temper is not fit to be entrusted with the responsibility of riding and schooling a young horse. Instead of educating and making it, they are ruining it, perhaps permanently.

When the horse has learnt to obey the rein aids, combine these with the leg aids. Continue using the schooling-whip as an aid to reinforce the leg until the horse is completely obedient.

Teach it the diagonal aids first before introducing the lateral aids—use of rein and leg on the same side. Always work equally on the left and right rein to prevent the horse becoming one-sided. Impulsion should always come from the hindquarters.

Once it has understood the rein and leg aids, ride it round the outdoor, or covered, school, on both the right and left rein.

The majority of horses seem to go more easily and freely to the left than to the right. So, unless one is careful, the natural tendency is to school them more on the left rein than on the right, making them stiffer on one side than the other, and unbalanced, and also the neck and shoulder muscles become more developed on one side than the other. To prevent this happening, the young horse should be schooled on both sides equally, or even a little more to the right, until it moves freely on both reins.

Always insist on the horse going right into the corners of the school; never let it cut its corners, whether walking or trotting. This supples it and teaches it to bend laterally; it also teaches it to go away from its rider's leg.

First ride it into the corners and make it halt facing the corner, standing correctly on all four legs. Then make it corner correctly, pushing its hindquarters round so that it pivots on its own centre. Practise this first from a walk, and then from a trot, making it halt correctly from both paces at the corners before turning. Do this on both the left and right rein, i.e., going round the *manège* to the left and the right.

Again, always insist on straight movement and even beats when walking forwards or backwards. When the horse understands and obeys, vary the number of paces in both directions.

THIRD STAGE   There is now no longer any need to have an assistant at the horse's head. This final stage is merely one of practising and perfecting the movement.

Teaching horse to rein back—third stage: rider giving aids, without assistant

It helps the horse to move straight backwards and forwards if one lays two rows of poles or *cavalletti* on the ground, parallel to each other and just wide enough apart for the horse to walk in between.

These act as guides, as the horse treads on them if it tries to turn its hindquarters out sideways.

Insist on its standing correctly at the end of each forward or backward movement, and upon it going smoothly into the rein-back, with hardly any pause after completing the forward movement. Also make it walk with even steps in both directions.

Gradually reduce the aids until they are practically invisible to an onlooker. The leg movement should be an almost imperceptible 'vibration' at the calf.

The amount of time each stage will take will entirely depend upon the individual horse and its ability and willingness to learn. But do not hurry at any of the stages, and do not go on to the next until the previous one has been thoroughly learnt.

In order to ensure straight movement when working without any poles on the ground as guide lines, choose some object directly ahead as a marker and keep your eyes on it when moving forwards or backwards. Stop immediately if the horse begins to swing its hindquarters sideways, and after straightening it make it walk forward again. Schooling alongside a fence is also a valuable help in keeping the horse moving straight, both forwards or backwards. Again vary the number of forward and backward steps, and gradually increase the latter.

Great patience is necessary. Young horses seem to learn this movement more easily than older ones, as might be expected, although I have successfully taught ponies aged seven or eight, who apparently had never previously been taught to rein back. I have always taught them by using the three progressive stages which I have described.

It is worse than useless merely to try to pull the horse backwards when mounted, as I have seen riders do when trying to make their horses rein back. When a horse is well schooled its rider's aids should be almost invisible to the onlooker.

It should also be possible to make a horse rein back even when it is being ridden in a head-collar or merely by using one's voice and the correct aids. My horses and ponies have been trained to do this, and very useful it is too when riding bareback up from the field to the stable, and when opening or shutting a gate.

The leg movement should gradually be reduced to a slight 'vibration' and squeeze, using the calves of the legs against the horse's sides behind the girth.

Once the horse has learnt to rein back correctly do not practise it too much, as this may encourage it to get behind the bit. When brought to a halt and asked to stand still it may anticipate a rein-back and start stepping backwards.

Trotting in circles to the left and right is a valuable exercise for suppling the young horse and making it respond to the leg aids, especially for teaching it to move away from the rider's leg. It also teaches it to bend laterally. The horse's head should always be kept turned inwards in the direction in which it is circling, as it is when lunged. In order to keep it balanced and even on both, trot equally on the right and left diagonals. If one always does a rising trot on the same diagonal, the horse feels uneven and uncomfortable when one trots on the other one. Ride first on the lunge rein and then without. Make the circles fairly large at first, gradually reducing them in size. The difficulty increases as the circles decrease in size.

Following directly on circling to the left and right is the figure of eight. This should be practised first walking and then trotting.

Again, begin with large circles, using about half the area of the *manège* or school for each circle, as decreasing their size increases their difficulty, especially when trotting. Practise riding the circles both at a sitting and at a rising trot. When doing a rising trot change the diagonals at the centre just before starting the new circle on the opposite rein. Ride on the left diagonal when circling to the left, and on the right when circling right. Then practise rising on the right diagonal when circling left, and *vice versa*. This will help to keep the horse balanced and even on both diagonals, and it will keep it alert.

Next teach the horse to canter on a circle; always make it lead with the correct foreleg, the left when cantering to the left and *vice versa*. Cantering on a circle when leading with the wrong leg can be dangerous as the horse can cross its legs and fall. Canter on a large circle at first. Always insist on a slow, collected canter; if the horse becomes excited and attempts to increase its pace or to play up, bring it back immediately to a trot or even a halt, and then start again.

Perhaps the best introduction to cantering on a circle is to practise at first riding on the lunge rein. Knot the reins and teach the horse to obey the voice and leg aids, to canter and then slow up to a trot, walk or halt. Use a neck-strap and if it disobeys pull on that rather than use the reins, and again give voice and leg aids. Canter equally on both circles, on or off the lunge.

The counter canter is a good suppling exercise and makes the horse use its shoulders. Teach it to canter to the right with its left leg leading or to the left with the right leg leading.

The counter canter must not be taught too soon in the horse's schooling in cantering, as it may make it lead with the wrong leg when doing an ordinary canter. And unless already fairly supple, it cannot perform it correctly. It may cause it to start changing legs behind, which is a very difficult fault to cure.

The best way of teaching the counter canter is to ride rather long and not very deep serpentines, or loops, at the canter. Canter in the school or alongside a fence with the right foreleg leading. Then come off the track and return to it while cantering, without changing the leading leg. Keep the horse bent to the right even when cantering to the left, as it must always bend towards the leading leg. Practise also to the left with the left foreleg leading.

As it becomes more supple, make the loops or serpentines increasingly deeper, until eventually the horse can counter canter right round the school, and in a complete circle; e.g., circle right with left foreleg leading and *vice versa*. Progress must be very gradual; correct movement is the most important thing.

It should never be allowed to canter false or disunited—what is called the 'butcher boy's canter'—with the leading hindleg on the opposite side to the leading foreleg.

When cantering united (or correctly) its leading foreleg and hindleg should be on the same side, and when cantering on the correct leg its head should be straightened up to the direction in which it is moving. If it breaks into a disunited canter, bring it back to a trot and start it cantering again correctly.

When the horse obeys the aids and can canter united, leading with the correct leg on both right and left circles, gradually decrease the size of the circles, and slightly decrease the pace. Only practise this on firm ground where there is no danger of the horse's legs slipping sideways from under it. Never practise on slippery ground.

Teach the horse to walk from the canter when quite sure that it will answer the aids given by your seat, and will relax its back muscles by using its hocks more actively. If it is at all stiff in the back the transition from a canter to a walk cannot be made correctly; the horse will resist and throw up its head, which is very bad for its schooling as it teaches it bad habits.

As a horse balances more easily at a canter if it is not moving in a straight line, begin schooling it on a fairly large circle. Keep it bent slightly towards its leading foreleg. Sit down into the saddle as deeply as possible while closing your legs; use very strong seat and back aids and resist with your hands; close your legs and push the horse's hindlegs increasingly under it until it is balanced, so that it can move straight from a canter into a walk.

In the early stages of training it will not be properly balanced and will have to trot for two or three steps.

Aids which are weak or not clear enough will make the horse come back to a walk with its weight thrown onto its forehand, making it feel heavy to the rider's hands.

The rider makes it canter increasingly slowly by lowering its croup, thus making the horse light to his hands. Only under these conditions can it move directly into a walk. Directly it does walk, relax the reins immediately and allow it to walk on freely with unrestricted movement.

When teaching the horse to canter a figure of eight, start it off on one circle at a slow, collected canter, leading with the correct inside foreleg. As it will have to lead with the opposite foreleg when cantering on the other circle, start by making it perform a simple change, having already taught it to change from a canter to a walk.

First teach it to lead with either leg as the rider directs, when cantering in a straight line, and make it move perfectly straight. Do not attempt a simple change so long as it throws its quarters in when starting to canter. By using his seat and inside leg as much as his outside leg, the rider can prevent the horse from pushing its quarters inwards when starting to canter.

Start cantering on the required leg; then make the horse perform a canter to a walk and walk on several paces before starting to canter with the other foreleg leading. The number of steps at the walk should gradually be reduced to only two or three before restarting to canter.

The change through a trot, which is used in dressage tests up to those of medium difficulty, is harder, and should be taught next, but only after much practice has been done on the simple change.

Start from the centre of the figure of eight and make both circles large. As the horse approaches the centre, again bring it back to a trot for about six steps, up to the centre point where it changes direction.

Then start cantering on the opposite circle, again leading with the correct inside foreleg.

Do not allow the horse to continue trotting once it starts moving on the opposite circle, but immediately make it start cantering. This requires considerable practice. Having achieved this, gradually reduce the number of steps until eventually only two are necessary at the centre where it changes direction. Finally try to reduce it to only one step, in order to change legs when changing from one circle to the other. Again do not attempt to hurry the training.

This is preliminary work in preparation for a flying-change, where a horse changes its legs in mid-air, when changing direction at the canter, from one circle to the other. This requires very accurate timing, on the rider's part, in shifting his weight in order to change the horse's balance from one leg to the other.

Insist on smooth transitions when changing pace from cantering to trotting, and again from trotting to cantering when starting the other circle.

When applying any aid at the trot, cease rising and sit down firmly in the saddle. This eventually becomes a preliminary signal to the horse that you are going to give a different aid.

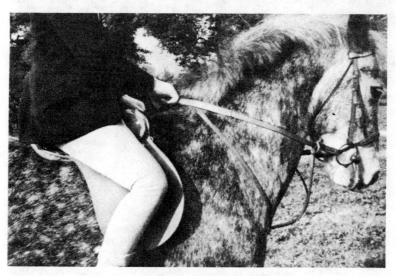

Neck-reining—position of rein on horse's neck. Note rider's hands

To teach the horse to neck-rein, apply the rein to one side fairly high up its neck towards its head. The lower down the rein is towards its wither the less influence it has. Do not pull your hand across its neck or push its head sideways with the rein, but merely apply light rein pressure against the side of its neck. Keep your hand low.

While neck-reining use your leg on the same side well behind the girth, and simultaneously shift your body weight over onto your seat bone on the side towards which you want the horse to turn. The rider's leg on the other side should be used at the girth to maintain impulsion and free forward movement. The leg and body merely reinforce the aid given by the rein. Eventually the horse should move in the required direction just by applying slight rein pressure to its neck, and slightly shifting the weight of your body. It should hardly be visible to the onlooker.

Bending—using rein and leg on same side

The Cutting horses in America, used for rounding up and roping steers, are trained to obey entirely by neck-reining. For example, when moving to the right: neck-rein with the left rein, use the left leg behind the girth and the right leg at the girth (to maintain impulsion). Body weight is shifted slightly over to the right. Reverse the aids when moving to the left.

When the horse is obedient to the neck-rein, bending it in either direction in and out of poles stuck in the ground (or even ten-gallon drums placed at intervals), with corresponding change of rein, is a valuable suppling exercise. Practise first at a walk, then at a trot and finally at a canter. As the pace increases, the distance between the poles (or drums) must be widened. Place them about ten feet apart at a walk, about fifteen feet apart when bending at a fast trot, and about twenty-two feet for a fairly fast canter.

In bending, the horse should move as close as possible to the poles or drums; the faster it is moving the closer it should go to them, so that its track resembles a serpentine or series of shallow loops— almost straight in fact—and just shaves the poles without touching them. In a bending race much time can be saved in this way, and a quick turn (on the proverbial 'sixpence') at the end for the return can also save time.

12 Elementary Dressage Continued

An important part of elementary dressage schooling is to gain control of the horse's haunches, so that it either moves or immobilizes its hindquarters at the rider's slightest indication.

The turn on the forehand is a valuable exercise for this purpose. Make the horse stand squarely on all four legs alongside, but not too close to, a wall or fence. Apply tension to the rein on the side on which you wish to turn, so that the horse's head moves in that direct-

Turn on the forehand, showing action of hindleg

Turn on the forehand, showing action of foreleg

ion until you can just see its eye. On no account force or wrench its head with the rein so that it is compelled to twist its neck round. While giving the rein aid, simultaneously draw back the inside leg and apply it with small 'vibrating' squeezes behind the girth. Use the outside leg at the girth to provide impulsion. This also stops the horse stepping backwards and prevents its hindquarters from swinging outwards.

To turn right on the forehand, turn the horse's head to the right just enough to make its right eye visible, and push its quarters round to the left, with the right leg drawn back behind the girth. The horse's off-foreleg either pivots or is picked up and replaced in the same place; the off-hindleg crosses over in front of the near-hindleg.

The horse must not step back, and it must certainly not step forward—this is a worse fault because it means that it has lost its

Pivot

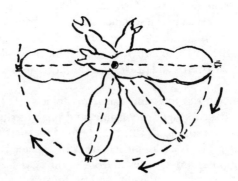

Turning right on the forehand

balance. Its head should remain still throughout the turn, which must be completed in one even movement. Reverse the aids to turn left on the forehand. The turn on the forehand is always performed from a halt.

At first only ask for quarter turns (90°), making four to a complete circle. Stand still after each turn and collect the horse before beginning the next turn. Balance the horse with the opposite rein as it completes a quarter turn to prevent it from moving too far round. At the end of four complete turns the horse's forelegs should be on the same spot as they were when it started. Paces should be even throughout each turn. Always follow four complete turns in one direction with four complete turns in the opposite direction.

When the horse has thoroughly mastered quarter turns on the forehand in both directions, practise half-turns (180°).

The turn on the forehand is simply an exercise to prove that the rider has gained control of the horse's haunches. Once the horse can do it successfully it need only be occasionally performed.

Having gained complete control of the horse's quarters through the turn on the forehand, turning on the haunches should not prove too difficult to teach.

The turn on the haunches is sometimes found in dressage tests, and is either performed from a halt or while moving. When executed at a halt the horse must first be made to stand correctly on all four legs. The hindleg on which it turns either pivots or is picked up and then replaced on the same spot.

As a preliminary exercise when teaching a horse to turn on the haunches from a halt, lay the rein against the horse's neck on the opposite side to which one wishes to turn. Make the horse walk briskly, or trot, in a small circle, using the outside leg behind the girth. Gradually decrease the size of the circle so that the horse walks in a spiral, until it is moving its forehand round its hindquarters. Make it walk with even steps without hesitating or stopping. Follow immediately by doing the same in the opposite direction.

For example, neck-rein with the left rein against the horse's neck. Keep the rein fairly high up its neck towards its head; if it is too low down near its wither, the rein's influence is lessened. Use the right rein to support the left. Use the left leg behind the girth to make the horse walk in a circle to the right, with the right leg at the girth to maintain impulsion. The left leg acts behind the girth to hold the

Pivot

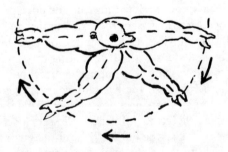

Turning right on the haunches

horse's quarters steady and prevent them from swinging out to the left. The horse walks to the right in gradually decreasing circles until its forehand is pivoting round on its haunches.

When turning to the left reverse the aids, using the right rein against the horse's neck and the right leg behind the girth.

Now repeat, using the same aids from a halt, i.e., without making the horse walk round in decreasing circles. Do four quarter (90°) turns, making the horse halt, standing correctly, between each. Collect it before beginning the next turn. Follow at once with four similar turns in the opposite direction. The hindlegs must be kept on the same spot throughout the movement.

If performed when moving, begin at the place indicated at a collected walk. The movement must be carried out with even steps, without any hesitating or stopping. Both forelegs must continue the walk steps without pivoting. In other words, the horse's forehand moves round its hindquarters; just the opposite to the turn on the forehand in which the hindquarters move round the forelegs. The horse should remain on the bit with a light rein contact. It must not step backwards, raise its head, or poke out its nose.

To turn on the haunches while moving is a difficult movement which needs much practice.

Gradually try to refine the aids until they become scarcely visible to an onlooker, both for the turn on the forehand and for the turn on the haunches.

13 Work on Two Tracks

Work on two tracks means that instead of the horse's hindfeet following in the tracks of its fore feet, it moves diagonally or laterally, with the forefeet crossing over on one track and the hindfeet doing the same thing on another.

The purpose of lateral work is to supple the horse's spine; it also makes the horse obedient to the aids and teaches it to go away from the rider's leg.

~oing away from its rider's leg

The easiest way of introducing a horse to the idea of diagonal movement, or work on two tracks, is up against a wall or fence. Ride it alongside the fence, open the inside rein in the direction of movement, and neck-rein with the outside rein. Push the horse's hindquarters round, with the outside leg well behind the girth so that it is no longer parallel with the fence but is facing diagonally towards it.

The horse when moving diagonally should pick up the outside foreleg and put it down over its inside foreleg. The outside hindleg similarly crosses over the inside hindleg.

Keep the horse moving steadily with plenty of impulsion, and insist on even steps. If it tries to back, push it forward again with both legs, or bring it back parallel to the fence and start again, meanwhile relaxing tension on the reins.

Insist on the horse moving its hindquarters over and do not allow it merely to walk forward with its body almost parallel to the fence and with its head and neck twisted sideways. Its body must move diagonally.

When the horse moves diagonally on two tracks with its head facing inwards it is called a shoulder-out.

Shoulder-out, to the right. Note rider's rein and leg aids and the horse's legs

When executing a shoulder-out to the left, open and lead with the left rein. Place the right rein against the horse's neck fairly near its head. Use the right leg strongly behind the girth to make it move away from your leg and turn its hindquarters diagonally. Shift your weight slightly to the left onto your left seat-bone.

Reverse the aids for a shoulder-out to the right.

The shoulder-in is another suppling movement which makes the horse bend its spine. It must be very supple to move correctly and daily practice keeps its muscles in good training.

It moves forward with its head, neck and shoulders following a

Shoulder-in, to the left

curve, the centre of which is the rider's outside leg; its hindlegs follow a parallel track to that made by its forelegs.

Ride parallel with the side of the *manège* and then turn the horse's forehand outwards off the track.

Open the outside rein and lead with it; use the inside rein against the horse's neck to give the flexion. The outside rein shows the way and also limits the direction of the movement.

The rider's outside leg, by acting strongly behind the girth, makes the horse's hindquarters move diagonally. The inside leg can act at the girth to maintain impulsion.

To ride a shoulder-in to the right, move parallel alongside the wall and then turn the horse's head to the right, off the track. Its head, neck and spine follow a curve which centres round your right leg.

Push the horse forward diagonally in this position with its right foreleg crossing over its left on one track, while its hindlegs do the same thing on an inner track. There must be free continuous movement with even steps.

Reverse the aids to perform a shoulder-in to the left.

The shoulder-out and shoulder-in are preparatory movements which should be learnt and perfected before the half-pass and full pass. They supple the horse, teach it to accept the bit, and keep its head steady. They also make it move freely with even steps (cadence), so that it is ready to start lateral work.

There are two ways of starting to teach the half-pass. It can either be initiated from a shoulder-in, or by riding in a half-circle and using the outside leg behind the girth to bring the horse back to the side of the wall on two tracks.

When beginning to teach the half-pass, do not allow the horse to try an evasion by throwing its weight onto its forehand, as it takes the first few steps on two tracks. Be content at first with a few side steps (say only two or three), gradually increasing the number as the horse begins to understand what is wanted, and becomes more proficient with practice. Stop immediately if it throws its weight onto its forehand. Bring the horse to a halt parallel with the wall and make it use its haunches more actively when it restarts the half-pass.

It is a valuable movement for making a horse go away from the rider's leg, and is one which is often useful, as for instance when bringing a horse alongside a gate to open or shut it. It forms a part of dressage tests to prove whether a horse obeys its rider's legs and hands.

Half-pass, to the left, across the school

Do not force the horse's head round, as this makes it resist and stiffen and causes uneven steps (loss of cadence). When it is bending correctly the horse should be looking slightly in the direction in which it is moving. As schooling progresses, become more strict and insist on the correct bend and head position, though at the beginning this is not so important as getting the horse to move forward freely with long, even strides. The inside legs are on the side to which the horse is bent and moving. The outside legs cross over in front of the inside legs, with the horse's body almost parallel to the side of the *manège*. Cadence (even steps) and free movement forward must be insisted upon. The horse must never be allowed to shorten its stride.

When employing the first method of starting to teach the half-pass, if performing it, for example, to the left, ride round the short side of the school. As you approach the long side make the horse shoulder-in to the left. This bends it in the correct position. Then use the right leg behind the girth, and as the left leg ceases to act the horse should move forward and towards the left.

When using the second method, by starting from a half-circle, use the outside leg behind the girth to bring the horse back on two tracks to the side of the school.

The next stage is to teach the horse to perform a half-pass diagonally across the school from one corner to the opposite corner. In doing this it must remain parallel to the long side of the school. This should be practised equally to the left and to the right. The cadence must be even and the pace must be kept steady and not allowed to slow down.

When first teaching the full pass, place the horse with its head and body in a straight line at right angles to the side of the school, with its head facing towards it. Open and lead with the inside rein to give direction, and press the outside rein against the horse's neck. The outside leg acts strongly behind the girth, to push the horse's hind-quarters sideways away from it. The rider's weight is shifted onto his inside seat bone on the side towards which the horse has to move.

The horse moves directly sideways at right angles to the side of the school, and parallel to the long side. Its forelegs move on one track and its hindlegs move on another, directly behind that made by the forelegs; there are two parallel tracks. The horse picks up its outside forefoot and crosses it over in front of the inside one. The outside hindfoot crosses over in front of the inside hindfoot.

For example, to perform a full pass to the right. Ride round the corner from the long, left side of the school. On coming to the short side make the horse start moving into a half-pass to the right. Then push its hindquarters sideways with the left leg acting strongly behind the girth, until the horse's head and body are facing at right angles towards the short side (i.e., the end) of the school. Open and lead with the right rein to give direction. Press the left rein against the horse's neck. The left leg acting strongly behind the girth pushes the horse's hindquarters sideways, away from it. The rider's weight is shifted onto his right seat bone as the horse is moving sideways to the right.

The horse picks up its left forefoot and crosses it over in front of its right. The left hindfoot is picked up and crosses over in front of the right hindfoot, directly behind the tracks made by the forefeet.

To ride a full pass to the left, come up the right-hand long side of the school towards the right-hand corner. Reverse the direction and the aids, so that the horse is moving directly sideways to the left, with its head and body again at right angles to the end (short side) of the school. The cadence should be even and the horse should move steadily sideways, without hesitating or stopping, for the required number of paces. Do not attempt too many steps, especially at first.

When the horse can perform a left or right half-pass perfectly at a walk, then one can begin to teach it this work on two tracks at a collected trot. The rider sits well down in the saddle. This is difficult work and great patience is needed as progress must not be hurried. Use the same aids, but there must be much greater impulsion. Cadence must be even with free forward movement. The horse must always be lightly on the bit. At first only expect to achieve two or three trot steps correctly performed, and only increase their number very gradually.

In a collected trot the horse raises its head so that its shoulders can move more freely. Its hocks must be well under it and active, although moving more slowly than in an ordinary trot. Although its steps are shorter the horse is lighter and more active than in an ordinary trot.

While performing these various dressage movements the horse should show no signs of nervousness or resistance. Grinding teeth and a swishing tail are both signs of unwillingness. The horse shows its obedience by slightly flexing its jaw while performing at all paces.

Difficult, advanced work cannot be attempted until absolute obedience is attained and all resistance by the horse has been reduced to the minimum. It must be completely relaxed, mentally and physically, and when it is the horse gives itself willingly and derives obvious pleasure in responding to the aids given by its rider. And its rigorous training will also have suppled the horse and developed its muscles. This should be the ultimate aim and object of all its schooling.

Both the habit of obedience and the training of the horse's muscles will go a long way to helping it to jump more easily and freely, and with fewer possibilities of it refusing. And the horse will be a far pleasanter ride in every way—it will be lighter and more balanced, and will move more smoothly at all paces.

The difference between riding a schooled and an unschooled horse might be compared with the difference between driving a high-powered, luxury sports car, with finger-tip control, and a lumbering old lorry.

I shall always remember the joy of riding a highly-schooled young Anglo-Arab. A touch on the reins and the slightest squeeze with one's knees was sufficient. If it had been given the treatment one sometimes sees meted out to unfortunate riding-school hacks, its rider would have been in the next county before he knew what had happened. Yet it was perfectly mannered and docile—if ridden in the right way. Its mouth was like silk and it could have been ridden on the proverbial pack-thread.

14 Boxing a Horse

One final and most important part in the education of a young horse is teaching it to enter a horsebox or trailer easily, and without any fuss. This part of its training should be undertaken as soon as possible. Just after it has been backed, while it is being quietly ridden about and accustomed to road traffic and other strange sights and sounds, would be as good a time as any (Chapter 8).

In fact, the younger it is when first introduced to the idea of being boxed, the better, within reason. And the less future trouble there is likely to be, provided that it is tackled in the right way.

If any horse or pony is once frightened and forced into a horsebox against its will, it will almost certainly be difficult, or practically impossible, to box ever again. There will be a fight and a struggle on each occasion and it will become progressively worse each time.

Yet, if the problem is approached in the correct way, the very first time, being boxed can become a normal, everyday occurrence to a horse or pony, and it will go in as easily as it enters its stable.

I have seen five people fail completely to persuade a hunter to be boxed, after four hours of exhausting and infuriating effort. Needless to say, it did *not* arrive at the Meet that day, much to its owner's annoyance.

I have also watched four large men trying to persuade a very small, unwilling pony to enter a trailer after a gymkhana. Although it was only about 11·2 hands high, it made them look extremely foolish. There was much shouting, waving of arms, flourishing of coats, and floods of bad language, all of which naturally made the wretched little pony more thoroughly frightened and bewildered than ever. Eventually it was dragged in, willy-nilly, by two men tugging at its head, while the other two pushed it up from behind, kicking lustily, with a rope round its hindquarters under its tail. My sympathies were all with the pony. Who would not have protested against such an affront to one's dignity?

First of all one must understand the horse's psychology and point of view. When confronted with a large and terrifying-looking contraption on wheels, with a dark interior and comparatively low and narrow opening, to say nothing of a steep, slippery and noisy ramp up which it is being invited to step, the horse's natural reaction is to resist. So the first essential is to overcome its natural fear, suspicion and dislike, and to persuade it that there is no possible danger. One must introduce the colt to the horsebox (or trailer) and reassure it that it is perfectly harmless.

Open the back of the horsebox and let down the ramp without the colt being present. Then fetch the colt and walk it round the box at a safe distance away, so that it can have a good look at it and become used to its appearance. Gradually bring the colt nearer until eventually it can be persuaded to go right up to it. When it does so, let it smell and examine it thoroughly, until it is completely satisfied that the monster has no evil intentions towards it. It will then probably turn away with a snort of contempt.

Then walk it round several times close to the box until it treats it with complete indifference. Put a thick layer of straw down on the ramp to deaden the clatter of its hooves when it walks up it. And put gates on each side so that it cannot slip off sideways, if it suddenly twists round when half-way up. This can be very dangerous. Besides terrifying it, it can easily break a leg if it falls off.

Place a bowl of oats invitingly at the bottom of the ramp and encourage the colt to eat the oats. If it has previously been kept without its breakfast, so much the better; it will be more likely to try to eat the oats. When it does so, place the bowl a little higher up the ramp, again just out of reach.

Persuade the colt to put one foot on the ramp. If it wants to, let it remove it again. Eventually greed or hunger will overcome fear and it will put both feet on in its efforts to reach the oats. When it does so allow it to eat for a little while, and then quietly place the bowl a little higher up, once more just out of reach.

In this way it will gradually mount the ramp, without any panic, its attention being concentrated on the food, until it reaches the entrance at the top. Then pick up the bowl and hold it out invitingly from just inside the box. It will probably enter, and the 'battle' has been won.

Alternatively, walk very slowly up the ramp holding the lead-rope in one hand and the bowl in the other, held out persuasively, just out of reach. Do not pull on the lead-rope. Provided that nothing startles it *en route*, eventually it can be coaxed up the ramp and persuaded to enter the box.

When it does so, make much of it, and give it a good feed inside the box. After it has finished eating lead it out down the ramp, and persuade it to enter again. Repeat this several times until it does so without any signs of fear or hesitation.

When this has been accomplished tie the colt up and let it eat some hay from the haynet already tied up in the box. Do not tie its head up too tightly, as it may resent this or suddenly panic, but give it a fairly long rope. If it suddenly panics at being tied up short it may start plunging and try to pull away. Leave it in for a short time, but keep close at hand. Talk to it and make much of it while it is tied.

I have successfully boxed a 'difficult' horse in this way, and the whole performance only took about half-an-hour. How much simpler than three or four hours vainly spent in trying to force it to go somewhere it didn't want to. If one tries using brute force with a horse one simply cannot win. Man's superior wits do not outwit the horse's infinitely greater strength.

As the dark interior may frighten the colt, either have the box facing the sun, or put a light inside it.

Be careful that it does not suddenly throw up its head and bang the top of it as it enters the box. This precaution is even more necessary with a trailer, especially if the horse is a tall one. Some horses seem to have a compulsive mania about passing under a low entrance. If they possibly can throw up their heads and bang them, they will.

It is often a good plan to lead a horse which boxes easily up the ramp first, in front of the colt. One horse will often follow another in without any difficulty.

It is worth while having a good deal of patience and taking a little time and trouble the first time a young horse is boxed, to train it to enter easily. How much better than having a Wild West performance, which one dreads, every time it has to travel. My own ponies have become so accustomed to being boxed that they all go up the ramp and enter with the utmost nonchalance.

When a horse travels, see that it has a deep bed of straw underfoot so that it cannot slip on the floor. The majority of horses and ponies seem to be good travellers and soon learn to balance themselves and go with the movement of the vehicle. Do not tie a horse's head up too short. If it did happen to overbalance it could break its neck if it fell. Always tie it up with a quick-release knot which pulls undone quickly and easily in an emergency. Try to tie it up so that its sides cannot be rubbed against the side of the box or trailer. There is more risk of this in a trailer as the horse's compartment is narrow, especially for a large animal. Always have a haynet tied up so that the horse can eat during the journey. This occupies its attention and helps to keep it calm and contented.

If two or more horses are travelling in a large horsebox, or in a cattle truck, they should be tied to the side so that they stand sideways, across the width of the box. Tie them head to tail, and put a barrier in between each so that they cannot start a quarrel and kick out at each other. If tied with their heads facing the same way, they may try to bite each other over the barriers. This inevitably leads to trouble.

On a long journey, take extra haynets and a bucket. Stop and water the horses, and lead them out to stretch their legs for a short time after about a couple of hours. Always stop to inspect them when a few miles out, to see whether they have settled down and are all right.

Some horses sweat quite considerably when travelling, especially if they are at all highly-strung. Take a rug, therefore, and cover a horse if it starts sweating badly, to prevent it from catching a chill by standing in a draught when damp. This is especially important in winter. In summer a light 'anti-sweat' rug (like a string vest) will be perfectly adequate.

Put knee-caps on the front legs for travelling. Bandage all four legs with woollen rest-bandages. To prevent the tail being rubbed, put on a tail-bandage, preferably with a tail-guard on top. This also prevents the tail-bandage from coming off, so that one does not find yards of filthy bandage trailing on the floor, and tangled round the horse's feet at the end of the journey.

If a horse is travelling by train it can either stand loose or between partitions which form a stall. If it is partitioned off, railway regulations insist on it wearing a head-collar and being tied up to a ring at head-level.

There are two schools of thought as to which method is the safer. Some think that it is dangerous for a horse to travel standing loose. They maintain that the swaying and jolting of the train may make it fall, and that if this happens it may injure itself while struggling to regain its feet. And if the box has to be shunted and it is done carelessly, there is particular risk of the horse falling. It should be given a really thick bed of wheat straw to provide a firm foothold. This lessens the risk of slipping or overbalancing. It also deadens the noise thus minimizing the risk of the horse becoming frightened.

On the other hand, others say that being partitioned off and tied up is more dangerous. The pony has no room to move and, if it slips, has therefore less chance of regaining its feet. Furthermore, should it fall, the jerk on the head-collar may break its neck, or it may choke, or be strangled.

Personally I incline to the second school of thought. Provided the horse has plenty of straw to stand on, I feel it runs less risk by travelling loose. As I have said already, most horses are usually good at balancing themselves, and soon learn to adapt themselves to the swaying of the train. And should the horse overbalance and fall it has less chance of hurting itself if there is plenty of straw on the floor to break its fall. And if it has a good foothold in the straw it has a better chance of regaining its feet, than if it were tied up. And it does not run the risk of having its neck broken, or being strangled or choked by a head-collar and rope.

Railway horseboxes have a groom's compartment. There is a small window through which one can watch the horse without disturbing it, and a door, for entering the box in an emergency. One should always travel in the groom's compartment with the horse, especially if it is a young one and likely to be frightened. The accommodation provided for the groom is not exactly luxurious, but one's personal comfort is a small consideration compared with the well-being of one's horse. Personally, I always travel with my ponies, and would never dream of doing anything else. If going by road I sit with the driver. It is also cheaper as it saves my own travelling expenses when going by road.

Also, if one accompanies a horse one can personally see that it has water and hay. One can also take some ready-mixed short feeds to be eaten *en route*, on a long trip.

Personal supervision of a horse's water and hay is essential, especially on a long railway journey. The railway authorities are supposed to arrange for horses, cattle and sheep to be watered and fed every two to three hours on the journey. But this does not always happen in practice, especially when travelling through the night. Cases have been known where a horse on a long journey has not been given any water or hay for twenty-four hours or more. Though, in fairness, I must say that I think those responsible are usually pretty conscientious, especially where a horse is concerned.

A horse should always be insured. Although it cannot bring a much-loved horse back to life in the event of an accident, it does mean that one receives some compensation, and can afford to buy another horse. The railway automatically insures it for a certain sum. Extra insurance over and above that costs approximately 7s 6d per £100. It is advisable to insure the horse for a considerable amount more than its actual money value—it makes the railways extra careful.

When hiring a horsebox always see that it is adequately covered by insurance. The risk of an accident on the road is too great to take any chances with one's horse. And if one possesses one's own trailer one should make quite certain that one is adequately protected, including third-party risks.

15 Summary of Training

Our young horse is fully trained at last. Five years of infinite patience, combined with hard but very rewarding work, have achieved this result. One has anxiously watched it grow and develop through all its stages, and now one has the pride and satisfaction of surveying one's handiwork and of knowing that it has been a job well done. One also has the joy of handling and riding the finished product and of enjoying the fruits of one's labours.

It has not all been plain sailing. The foal has had a developing mind, will and character of its own. These, one has not sought to break or destroy, but to mould so that the young horse has finally become an ornament to the equine race.

There have been moments of anxiety, frustration and possibly even of despair. There may have been periods when progress seemed to be painfully slow, or even when one appeared to be making no headway at all. Perhaps the foal or colt has played up at times, or has gone through a phase of wilfulness, or apparent obstinacy. Or maybe one has had to go right back to the beginning, after one thought it had learnt some lesson and then found that it had not. Possibly one has forced the pace too much at some particular stage, in one's over-enthusiasm and anxiety to achieve results. One has probably made mistakes oneself, for which the young pupil has suffered.

And if one starts training another foal, one will probably have an entirely different set of problems with which to contend—no two horses are alike in character or temperament. So one faces a new challenge with every different horse or pony that one handles and rides, or schools.

One of the fascinations of handling horses and of riding is that one has never finished learning. Several lives would not be too long in which to learn all one should know about stable management, schooling, show-jumping, combined training, dressage, or even just ordinary riding. One never reaches the ultimate goal.

If one has climbed to the top of Mount Everest, that is it. There are no higher mountains left in the world to climb. But with horses, there is always some higher peak to reach, away on the horizon. The schooling and work in dressage so far described are by no means the end. They are merely the foundation upon which the ambitious can go on and continue to build. For instance, there is *Haute École*, or High School, which opens out whole vast new fields of schooling. There are also show-jumping, one- and three-day events, to test a horse's versatility, and there is showing. All these require specialized training and schooling, for both horse and rider.

Not all horses have the conformation, temperament, or mental capacity to progress very far beyond the stage reached in this book. In fact, it is fairly safe to say that horses which have the potential ability (including character and temperament), are few and far between. And even if one is lucky enough to possess one which has, it takes years to train it up to this pitch of perfection. And if it has not, then the attempt to do so can only end in failure and disappointment to the owner, through no fault of the horse.

Nor is every rider capable, physically or mentally, of reaching the heights and becoming a great horseman, or woman. Just as potential *Haute École* horses are rare, so also are riders who are capable of achieving this standard of equitation. That is why there is only a handful of Olympic riders of world class, in all the nations combined.

It requires a rider of exceptional ability, knowledge and experience, and years of training are needed. Anyone who feels that they have the ability and wishes to scale these heights, must have both the time and money to be able to devote themselves entirely to it. And they must be completely dedicated. It is a vocation, and a life-work. And a very hard life at that.

This book is not intended for them, but for those who want to have the pleasure and satisfaction of schooling their own young horse up to the stage when it will be a companion with whom they can share many happy hours, and have a tremendous amount of fun.

I, for one, do not pretend to be able to go beyond this stage, having never had the opportunity, nor having the money, time, knowledge and experience that is necessary. And even if I had, I could probably never do it. So why worry? I love my ponies, and I thoroughly enjoy every moment that I am with them, whether in the stable, or when riding. And that is all that really matters. And I think I have been able to give the same happiness to many of my pupils. That is my reward, and the satisfaction I gain from a life spent with horses and ponies.

For those who want to progress further, I recommend them to

study *Equitation* by H. Wynmalen, published by *Country Life* in 1952, especially the chapters on Advanced and High-School Riding.

The following article, reproduced by courtesy of *Horse and Hound*, appeared in that periodical in November, 1966, some time after this book was written. As it is by that great authority, Colonel V. D. S. Williams, I have included it here, because I feel that it supports the main principles which I have tried to explain. Note particularly what Col. Williams has written about the gap between Phase 2 and Phase 3, and compare this with what I have written in Chapter 15. The Introduction to The British Horse Society's *Notes on Dressage* deserves the most careful study.

Beware of False Prophets! *They harm the cause of dressage.* A serious misconception still exists as to the real purpose and value of dressage—but is it altogether the fault of the 'leading exponents'?

The introduction to the first edition of the British Horse Society's *Notes on Dressage* which, as chairman of the then newly-appointed committee, I wrote nearly 20 years ago, has appeared in subsequent editions without any change, and is reproduced on page 106.

Unfortunately there are many false prophets who, because they have achieved some success in equestrian activities, carry too much weight in the dressage world and, by trying to obtain quick results, present a false picture of dressage.

We have always taught that there are three phases of dressage:

PHASE 1   Riding the horse with a natural carriage in free forward movements. In this phase the horse becomes accustomed to the weight of the rider, adjusts his balance accordingly, learns to carry himself without leaning on the reins and becomes accustomed to the elementary aids.

This stage, which should be achieved in about a year, is probably quite sufficient for the rider who merely wants to enjoy his hunting and hacking and have a sound horse.

PHASE 2   This is known on the Continent as the Campagne School. It consists of riding the collected horse in certain school movements, such as turns, circles, etc., in perfect balance. This can only be carried out if the first phase has been correctly performed.

This phase, which should be achieved by the end of the second year, is important to those riders who wish to take part in competitions such as show-jumping, combined training events, show riding, especially of hacks, and requires that the rider has considerably more knowledge and time at his disposal than for the first stage.

PHASE 3 This includes *Haute École*, and is for the expert only and quite outside the range of the ordinary rider. It requires a vast amount of time and experience and is not likely to be achieved under at least three years' intensive training and is impossible without a proper preparation in phases 1 and 2.

If this is attempted by people who have not the time and experience, nothing but bad results can be expected.

Most of these bad results are generally carried out by riders who have neglected phase 1 and tried by short cuts to enter their horses for competitions for which they are not ready.

There is a distinct difference between the 'Classical Dressage' riders and what might be called the 'Entertainers'.

The latter are generally brilliant natural horsemen, who can achieve spectacular results which are most entertaining to the public, but from the economic point of view, they often cannot afford the time to make their work truly classical.

This gift, had it been concentrated on classical dressage, would probably have produced Olympic champions.

Although there is much to be learned from these experts, it is most dangerous for the ordinary rider to try to follow their methods.

If the ordinary rider would confine himself to phases 1 and 2 and only compete in dressage tests for which his horse is ready, there would not be so many of those unfortunate exhibitions which do so much harm to the cause.

THE WISDOM OF 20 YEARS AGO

The following introduction to the British Horse Society's Notes on Dressage *was written by Col. V. D. S. Williams for the first edition nearly 20 years ago. It has remained unchanged in all subsequent editions.*

Until there is a more thorough understanding in this country of the meaning of the word 'Dressage' with regard to the training of the riding horse, there will be no marked improvement in the training of our hunters, hacks, polo ponies and children's ponies.

The word itself, being foreign, has proved somewhat of a stumbling-block, but it is difficult to find a word in English to take its place.

Dressage signifies the training of the horse for riding for pleasure as opposed to the training of the horse for the race-course, although the latter would, in all probability, benefit if dressage were introduced into its early training as well.

It would appear, therefore, that this word must be incorporated into the English language, in common with so many other French words such as 'chauffeur', which signifies the driver of a private car as opposed to the driver of a lorry or bus.

It must be understood that a covered riding-school or an open air *manège* are not essentials. They are undoubtedly of great assistance, the former especially in the winter months, but as long as a flat piece of ground is available where the going is good and a fence along at least one side of it, to give direction, very excellent results can be obtained.

There is also a misconception which is prevalent among riding people, namely, that the object of dressage is to prepare horses for tests—that is entirely wrong.

One does not learn to read and write in order to take part in examinations. Examinations have their use in testing the progress that is being made.

It is the same with dressage tests, they are of value in ascertaining the progress that is being made in the training and in comparing the ability of one individual (horse or rider) against another.

The true purpose of dressage is to improve the standard of training of the riding horse and to provide a progressive system which will teach the horse to balance himself with the weight of his rider, without putting undue strain on any sets of joints or muscles, thus enabling him to comply easily and happily with the demands of his rider and to improve his paces and bearing.

The whole secret of dressage lies in placing the horse's head in the right position by controlling the hindlegs. It is the rider's legs and seat that must be the chief influence in placing the horse's head, and a snaffle bridle is the only bit for the purpose.

If an attempt is made to pull the horse's head into position with a double bridle, the mouth would inevitably be ruined and the action impaired.

The double bridle should not be used until the position of the head is established.

The horse must be made to go forward by the hindlegs propelling the forelegs immediately in front of them.

He must be taught to increase and decrease his stride in all paces without altering the rhythm.

He must be taught the lateral movements, not only to enable him to go on two tracks, but in order to overcome evasions, to supple the spine, to teach the horse to be obedient to the rider's legs and to keep the horse straight.

The greatest difficulty in equitation is to keep the horse straight.

Index

A PERSONAL WORD FROM MELVIN POWERS
PUBLISHER, WILSHIRE BOOK COMPANY

Dear Friend:

My goal is to publish interesting, informative, and inspirational books. You can help me accomplish this by answering the following questions, either by phone or by mail. Or, if convenient for you, I would welcome the opportunity to visit with you in my office and hear your comments in person.

Did you enjoy reading this book? Why?

Would you enjoy reading another similar book?

What idea in the book impressed you the most?

If applicable to your situation, have you incorporated this idea in your daily life?

Is there a chapter that could serve as a theme for an entire book? Please explain.

If you have an idea for a book, I would welcome discussing it with you. If you already have one in progress, write or call me concerning possible publication. I can be reached at (213) 875-1711 or (818) 983-1105.

Sincerely yours,

MELVIN POWERS

12015 Sherman Road
North Hollywood, California 91605

MELVIN POWERS SELF-IMPROVEMENT LIBRARY

ASTROLOGY

_____ ASTROLOGY: HOW TO CHART YOUR HOROSCOPE *Max Heindel*	5.00
_____ ASTROLOGY AND SEXUAL ANALYSIS *Morris C. Goodman*	5.00
_____ ASTROLOGY MADE EASY *Astarte*	5.00
_____ ASTROLOGY, ROMANCE, YOU AND THE STARS *Anthony Norvell*	5.00
_____ MY WORLD OF ASTROLOGY *Sydney Omarr*	7.00
_____ THOUGHT DIAL *Sydney Omarr*	4.00
_____ WHAT THE STARS REVEAL ABOUT THE MEN IN YOUR LIFE *Thelma White*	3.00

BRIDGE

_____ BRIDGE BIDDING MADE EASY *Edwin B. Kantar*	10.00
_____ BRIDGE CONVENTIONS *Edwin B. Kantar*	7.00
_____ BRIDGE HUMOR *Edwin B. Kantar*	5.00
_____ COMPETITIVE BIDDING IN MODERN BRIDGE *Edgar Kaplan*	7.00
_____ DEFENSIVE BRIDGE PLAY COMPLETE *Edwin B. Kantar*	15.00
_____ GAMESMAN BRIDGE—Play Better with Kantar *Edwin B. Kantar*	5.00
_____ HOW TO IMPROVE YOUR BRIDGE *Alfred Sheinwold*	5.00
_____ IMPROVING YOUR BIDDING SKILLS *Edwin B. Kantar*	4.00
_____ INTRODUCTION TO DECLARER'S PLAY *Edwin B. Kantar*	5.00
_____ INTRODUCTION TO DEFENDER'S PLAY *Edwin B. Kantar*	5.00
_____ KANTAR FOR THE DEFENSE *Edwin B. Kantar*	7.00
_____ KANTAR FOR THE DEFENSE VOLUME 2 *Edwin B. Kantar*	7.00
_____ SHORT CUT TO WINNING BRIDGE *Alfred Sheinwold*	3.00
_____ TEST YOUR BRIDGE PLAY *Edwin B. Kantar*	5.00
_____ VOLUME 2—TEST YOUR BRIDGE PLAY *Edwin B. Kantar*	5.00
_____ WINNING DECLARER PLAY *Dorothy Hayden Truscott*	7.00

BUSINESS, STUDY & REFERENCE

_____ CONVERSATION MADE EASY *Elliot Russell*	4.00
_____ EXAM SECRET *Dennis B. Jackson*	3.00
_____ FIX-IT BOOK *Arthur Symons*	2.00
_____ HOW TO DEVELOP A BETTER SPEAKING VOICE *M. Hellier*	4.00
_____ HOW TO SELF-PUBLISH YOUR BOOK & MAKE IT A BEST SELLER *Melvin Powers*	10.00
_____ INCREASE YOUR LEARNING POWER *Geoffrey A. Dudley*	3.00
_____ PRACTICAL GUIDE TO BETTER CONCENTRATION *Melvin Powers*	3.00
_____ PRACTICAL GUIDE TO PUBLIC SPEAKING *Maurice Forley*	5.00
_____ 7 DAYS TO FASTER READING *William S. Schaill*	5.00
_____ SONGWRITERS' RHYMING DICTIONARY *Jane Shaw Whitfield*	7.00
_____ SPELLING MADE EASY *Lester D. Basch & Dr. Milton Finkelstein*	3.00
_____ STUDENT'S GUIDE TO BETTER GRADES *J. A. Rickard*	3.00
_____ TEST YOURSELF—Find Your Hidden Talent *Jack Shafer*	3.00
_____ YOUR WILL & WHAT TO DO ABOUT IT *Attorney Samuel G. Kling*	5.00

CALLIGRAPHY

_____ ADVANCED CALLIGRAPHY *Katherine Jeffares*	7.00
_____ CALLIGRAPHER'S REFERENCE BOOK *Anne Leptich & Jacque Evans*	7.00
_____ CALLIGRAPHY—The Art of Beautiful Writing *Katherine Jeffares*	7.00
_____ CALLIGRAPHY FOR FUN & PROFIT *Anne Leptich & Jacque Evans*	7.00
_____ CALLIGRAPHY MADE EASY *Tina Serafini*	7.00

CHESS & CHECKERS

_____ BEGINNER'S GUIDE TO WINNING CHESS *Fred Reinfeld*	5.00
_____ CHESS IN TEN EASY LESSONS *Larry Evans*	5.00
_____ CHESS MADE EASY *Milton L. Hanauer*	3.00
_____ CHESS PROBLEMS FOR BEGINNERS *edited by Fred Reinfeld*	5.00
_____ CHESS SECRETS REVEALED *Fred Reinfeld*	2.00
_____ CHESS TACTICS FOR BEGINNERS *edited by Fred Reinfeld*	5.00
_____ CHESS THEORY & PRACTICE *Morry & Mitchell*	2.00
_____ HOW TO WIN AT CHECKERS *Fred Reinfeld*	3.00
_____ 1001 BRILLIANT WAYS TO CHECKMATE *Fred Reinfeld*	5.00
_____ 1001 WINNING CHESS SACRIFICES & COMBINATIONS *Fred Reinfeld*	5.00

_____ SOVIET CHESS *Edited by R. G. Wade*   3.00

COOKERY & HERBS

_____ CULPEPER'S HERBAL REMEDIES *Dr. Nicholas Culpeper*   3.00
_____ FAST GOURMET COOKBOOK *Poppy Cannon*   2.50
_____ GINSENG The Myth & The Truth *Joseph P. Hou*   3.00
_____ HEALING POWER OF HERBS *May Bethel*   4.00
_____ HEALING POWER OF NATURAL FOODS *May Bethel*   5.00
_____ HERB HANDBOOK *Dawn MacLeod*   3.00
_____ HERBS FOR HEALTH—How to Grow & Use Them *Louise Evans Doole*   4.00
_____ HOME GARDEN COOKBOOK—Delicious Natural Food Recipes *Ken Kraft*   3.00
_____ MEDICAL HERBALIST *edited by Dr. J. R. Yemm*   3.00
_____ VEGETABLE GARDENING FOR BEGINNERS *Hugh Wiberg*   2.00
_____ VEGETABLES FOR TODAY'S GARDENS *R. Milton Carleton*   2.00
_____ VEGETARIAN COOKERY *Janet Walker*   7.00
_____ VEGETARIAN COOKING MADE EASY & DELECTABLE *Veronica Vezza*   3.00
_____ VEGETARIAN DELIGHTS—A Happy Cookbook for Health *K. R. Mehta*   2.00
_____ VEGETARIAN GOURMET COOKBOOK *Joyce McKinnel*   3.00

GAMBLING & POKER

_____ ADVANCED POKER STRATEGY & WINNING PLAY *A. D. Livingston*   5.00
_____ HOW TO WIN AT DICE GAMES *Skip Frey*   3.00
_____ HOW TO WIN AT POKER *Terence Reese & Anthony T. Watkins*   5.00
_____ WINNING AT CRAPS *Dr. Lloyd T. Commins*   4.00
_____ WINNING AT GIN *Chester Wander & Cy Rice*   3.00
_____ WINNING AT POKER—An Expert's Guide *John Archer*   5.00
_____ WINNING AT 21—An Expert's Guide *John Archer*   5.00
_____ WINNING POKER SYSTEMS *Norman Zadeh*   3.00

HEALTH

_____ BEE POLLEN *Lynda Lyngheim & Jack Scagnetti*   3.00
_____ DR. LINDNER'S SPECIAL WEIGHT CONTROL METHOD *P. G. Lindner, M.D.*   2.00
_____ HELP YOURSELF TO BETTER SIGHT *Margaret Darst Corbett*   3.00
_____ HOW YOU CAN STOP SMOKING PERMANENTLY *Ernest Caldwell*   5.00
_____ MIND OVER PLATTER *Peter G. Lindner, M.D.*   3.00
_____ NATURE'S WAY TO NUTRITION & VIBRANT HEALTH *Robert J. Scrutton*   3.00
_____ NEW CARBOHYDRATE DIET COUNTER *Patti Lopez-Pereira*   2.00
_____ REFLEXOLOGY *Dr. Maybelle Segal*   4.00
_____ REFLEXOLOGY FOR GOOD HEALTH *Anna Kaye & Don C. Matchan*   5.00
_____ 30 DAYS TO BEAUTIFUL LEGS *Dr. Marc Selner*   3.00
_____ YOU CAN LEARN TO RELAX *Dr. Samuel Gutwirth*   3.00
_____ YOUR ALLERGY—What To Do About It *Allan Knight, M.D.*   3.00

HOBBIES

_____ BEACHCOMBING FOR BEGINNERS *Norman Hickin*   2.00
_____ BLACKSTONE'S MODERN CARD TRICKS *Harry Blackstone*   5.00
_____ BLACKSTONE'S SECRETS OF MAGIC *Harry Blackstone*   5.00
_____ COIN COLLECTING FOR BEGINNERS *Burton Hobson & Fred Reinfeld*   5.00
_____ ENTERTAINING WITH ESP *Tony 'Doc' Shiels*   2.00
_____ 400 FASCINATING MAGIC TRICKS YOU CAN DO *Howard Thurston*   5.00
_____ HOW I TURN JUNK INTO FUN AND PROFIT *Sari*   3.00
_____ HOW TO WRITE A HIT SONG & SELL IT *Tommy Boyce*   7.00
_____ JUGGLING MADE EASY *Rudolf Dittrich*   3.00
_____ MAGIC FOR ALL AGES *Walter Gibson*   4.00
_____ MAGIC MADE EASY *Byron Wels*   2.00
_____ STAMP COLLECTING FOR BEGINNERS *Burton Hobson*   3.00

HORSE PLAYERS' WINNING GUIDES

_____ BETTING HORSES TO WIN *Les Conklin*   5.00
_____ ELIMINATE THE LOSERS *Bob McKnight*   5.00
_____ HOW TO PICK WINNING HORSES *Bob McKnight*   5.00
_____ HOW TO WIN AT THE RACES *Sam (The Genius) Lewin*   5.00
_____ HOW YOU CAN BEAT THE RACES *Jack Kavanagh*   5.00

____ MAKING MONEY AT THE RACES *David Barr*		5.00
____ PAYDAY AT THE RACES *Les Conklin*		5.00
____ SMART HANDICAPPING MADE EASY *William Bauman*		5.00
____ SUCCESS AT THE HARNESS RACES *Barry Meadow*		5.00
____ WINNING AT THE HARNESS RACES—An Expert's Guide *Nick Cammarano*		5.00

HUMOR

____ HOW TO FLATTEN YOUR TUSH *Coach Marge Reardon*	2.00
____ HOW TO MAKE LOVE TO YOURSELF *Ron Stevens & Joy Grdnic*	3.00
____ JOKE TELLER'S HANDBOOK *Bob Orben*	5.00
____ JOKES FOR ALL OCCASIONS *Al Schock*	5.00
____ 2000 NEW LAUGHS FOR SPEAKERS *Bob Orben*	5.00
____ 2,500 JOKES TO START 'EM LAUGHING *Bob Orben*	5.00

HYPNOTISM

____ ADVANCED TECHNIQUES OF HYPNOSIS *Melvin Powers*	3.00
____ BRAINWASHING AND THE CULTS *Paul A. Verdier, Ph.D.*	3.00
____ CHILDBIRTH WITH HYPNOSIS *William S. Kroger, M.D.*	5.00
____ HOW TO SOLVE Your Sex Problems with Self-Hypnosis *Frank S. Caprio, M.D.*	5.00
____ HOW TO STOP SMOKING THRU SELF-HYPNOSIS *Leslie M. LeCron*	3.00
____ HOW TO USE AUTO-SUGGESTION EFFECTIVELY *John Duckworth*	3.00
____ HOW YOU CAN BOWL BETTER USING SELF-HYPNOSIS *Jack Heise*	4.00
____ HOW YOU CAN PLAY BETTER GOLF USING SELF-HYPNOSIS *Jack Heise*	3.00
____ HYPNOSIS AND SELF-HYPNOSIS *Bernard Hollander, M.D.*	5.00
____ HYPNOTISM *(Originally published in 1893) Carl Sextus*	5.00
____ HYPNOTISM & PSYCHIC PHENOMENA *Simeon Edmunds*	4.00
____ HYPNOTISM MADE EASY *Dr. Ralph Winn*	5.00
____ HYPNOTISM MADE PRACTICAL *Louis Orton*	5.00
____ HYPNOTISM REVEALED *Melvin Powers*	3.00
____ HYPNOTISM TODAY *Leslie LeCron and Jean Bordeaux, Ph.D.*	5.00
____ MODERN HYPNOSIS *Lesley Kuhn & Salvatore Russo, Ph.D.*	5.00
____ NEW CONCEPTS OF HYPNOSIS *Bernard C. Gindes, M.D.*	7.00
____ NEW SELF-HYPNOSIS *Paul Adams*	7.00
____ POST-HYPNOTIC INSTRUCTIONS—Suggestions for Therapy *Arnold Furst*	5.00
____ PRACTICAL GUIDE TO SELF-HYPNOSIS *Melvin Powers*	3.00
____ PRACTICAL HYPNOTISM *Philip Magonet, M.D.*	3.00
____ SECRETS OF HYPNOTISM *S. J. Van Pelt, M.D.*	5.00
____ SELF-HYPNOSIS A Conditioned-Response Technique *Laurence Sparks*	7.00
____ SELF-HYPNOSIS Its Theory, Technique & Application *Melvin Powers*	3.00
____ THERAPY THROUGH HYPNOSIS *edited by Raphael H. Rhodes*	5.00

JUDAICA

____ SERVICE OF THE HEART *Evelyn Garfiel, Ph.D.*	7.00
____ STORY OF ISRAEL IN COINS *Jean & Maurice Gould*	2.00
____ STORY OF ISRAEL IN STAMPS *Maxim & Gabriel Shamir*	1.00
____ TONGUE OF THE PROPHETS *Robert St. John*	7.00

JUST FOR WOMEN

____ COSMOPOLITAN'S GUIDE TO MARVELOUS MEN Fwd. by *Helen Gurley Brown*	3.00
____ COSMOPOLITAN'S HANG-UP HANDBOOK Foreword by *Helen Gurley Brown*	4.00
____ COSMOPOLITAN'S LOVE BOOK—A Guide to Ecstasy in Bed	7.00
____ COSMOPOLITAN'S NEW ETIQUETTE GUIDE Fwd. by *Helen Gurley Brown*	4.00
____ I AM A COMPLEAT WOMAN *Doris Hagopian & Karen O'Connor Sweeney*	3.00
____ JUST FOR WOMEN—A Guide to the Female Body *Richard E. Sand, M.D.*	5.00
____ NEW APPROACHES TO SEX IN MARRIAGE *John E. Eichenlaub, M.D.*	3.00
____ SEXUALLY ADEQUATE FEMALE *Frank S. Caprio, M.D.*	3.00
____ SEXUALLY FULFILLED WOMAN *Dr. Rachel Copelan*	5.00
____ YOUR FIRST YEAR OF MARRIAGE *Dr. Tom McGinnis*	3.00

MARRIAGE, SEX & PARENTHOOD

____ ABILITY TO LOVE *Dr. Allan Fromme*	7.00
____ GUIDE TO SUCCESSFUL MARRIAGE *Drs. Albert Ellis & Robert Harper*	7.00
____ HOW TO RAISE AN EMOTIONALLY HEALTHY, HAPPY CHILD *A. Ellis*	5.00

_____ SEX WITHOUT GUILT *Albert Ellis, Ph.D.*		5.00
_____ SEXUALLY ADEQUATE MALE *Frank S. Caprio, M.D.*		3.00
_____ SEXUALLY FULFILLED MAN *Dr. Rachel Copelan*		5.00
_____ STAYING IN LOVE *Dr. Norton F. Kristy*		7.00

MELVIN POWERS' MAIL ORDER LIBRARY

_____ HOW TO GET RICH IN MAIL ORDER *Melvin Powers*		20.00
_____ HOW TO WRITE A GOOD ADVERTISEMENT *Victor O. Schwab*		20.00
_____ MAIL ORDER MADE EASY *J. Frank Brumbaugh*		20.00

METAPHYSICS & OCCULT

_____ BOOK OF TALISMANS, AMULETS & ZODIACAL GEMS *William Pavitt*		7.00
_____ CONCENTRATION—A Guide to Mental Mastery *Mouni Sadhu*		5.00
_____ EXTRA-TERRESTRIAL INTELLIGENCE—The First Encounter		6.00
_____ FORTUNE TELLING WITH CARDS *P. Foli*		5.00
_____ HOW TO INTERPRET DREAMS, OMENS & FORTUNE TELLING SIGNS *Gettings*		5.00
_____ HOW TO UNDERSTAND YOUR DREAMS *Geoffrey A. Dudley*		5.00
_____ ILLUSTRATED YOGA *William Zorn*		3.00
_____ IN DAYS OF GREAT PEACE *Mouni Sadhu*		3.00
_____ LSD—THE AGE OF MIND *Bernard Roseman*		2.00
_____ MAGICIAN—His Training and Work *W. E. Butler*		3.00
_____ MEDITATION *Mouni Sadhu*		7.00
_____ MODERN NUMEROLOGY *Morris C. Goodman*		5.00
_____ NUMEROLOGY—ITS FACTS AND SECRETS *Ariel Yvon Taylor*		3.00
_____ NUMEROLOGY MADE EASY *W. Mykian*		5.00
_____ PALMISTRY MADE EASY *Fred Gettings*		5.00
_____ PALMISTRY MADE PRACTICAL *Elizabeth Daniels Squire*		5.00
_____ PALMISTRY SECRETS REVEALED *Henry Frith*		4.00
_____ PROPHECY IN OUR TIME *Martin Ebon*		2.50
_____ SUPERSTITION—Are You Superstitious? *Eric Maple*		2.00
_____ TAROT *Mouni Sadhu*		10.00
_____ TAROT OF THE BOHEMIANS *Papus*		7.00
_____ WAYS TO SELF-REALIZATION *Mouni Sadhu*		7.00
_____ WITCHCRAFT, MAGIC & OCCULTISM—A Fascinating History *W. B. Crow*		7.00
_____ WITCHCRAFT—THE SIXTH SENSE *Justine Glass*		7.00
_____ WORLD OF PSYCHIC RESEARCH *Hereward Carrington*		2.00

SELF-HELP & INSPIRATIONAL

_____ CHARISMA How To Get "That Special Magic" *Marcia Grad*		7.00
_____ DAILY POWER FOR JOYFUL LIVING *Dr. Donald Curtis*		5.00
_____ DYNAMIC THINKING *Melvin Powers*		5.00
_____ GREATEST POWER IN THE UNIVERSE *U. S. Andersen*		7.00
_____ GROW RICH WHILE YOU SLEEP *Ben Sweetland*		7.00
_____ GROWTH THROUGH REASON *Albert Ellis, Ph.D.*		7.00
_____ GUIDE TO PERSONAL HAPPINESS *Albert Ellis, Ph.D. & Irving Becker, Ed. D.*		7.00
_____ HANDWRITING ANALYSIS MADE EASY *John Marley*		5.00
_____ HANDWRITING TELLS *Nadya Olyanova*		7.00
_____ HELPING YOURSELF WITH APPLIED PSYCHOLOGY *R. Henderson*		2.00
_____ HOW TO ATTRACT GOOD LUCK *A. H. Z. Carr*		7.00
_____ HOW TO BE GREAT *Dr. Donald Curtis*		5.00
_____ HOW TO DEVELOP A WINNING PERSONALITY *Martin Panzer*		5.00
_____ HOW TO DEVELOP AN EXCEPTIONAL MEMORY *Young & Gibson*		5.00
_____ HOW TO LIVE WITH A NEUROTIC *Albert Ellis, Ph. D.*		5.00
_____ HOW TO OVERCOME YOUR FEARS *M. P. Leahy, M.D.*		3.00
_____ HOW TO SUCCEED *Brian Adams*		7.00
_____ HUMAN PROBLEMS & HOW TO SOLVE THEM *Dr. Donald Curtis*		5.00
_____ I CAN *Ben Sweetland*		7.00
_____ I WILL *Ben Sweetland*		3.00
_____ KNIGHT IN THE RUSTY ARMOR *Robert Fisher*		10.00
_____ LEFT-HANDED PEOPLE *Michael Barsley*		5.00
_____ MAGIC IN YOUR MIND *U. S. Andersen*		7.00

____ MAGIC OF THINKING BIG *Dr. David J. Schwartz*		3.00
____ MAGIC OF THINKING SUCCESS *Dr. David J. Schwartz*		7.00
____ MAGIC POWER OF YOUR MIND *Walter M. Germain*		7.00
____ MENTAL POWER THROUGH SLEEP SUGGESTION *Melvin Powers*		3.00
____ NEVER UNDERESTIMATE THE SELLING POWER OF A WOMAN *Dottie Walters*		7.00
____ NEW GUIDE TO RATIONAL LIVING *Albert Ellis, Ph.D. & R. Harper, Ph.D.*		7.00
____ PROJECT YOU *A Manual of Rational Assertiveness Training Paris & Casey*		6.00
____ PSYCHO-CYBERNETICS *Maxwell Maltz, M.D.*		5.00
____ PSYCHOLOGY OF HANDWRITING *Nadya Olyanova*		7.00
____ SALES CYBERNETICS *Brian Adams*		7.00
____ SCIENCE OF MIND IN DAILY LIVING *Dr. Donald Curtis*		7.00
____ SECRET OF SECRETS *U. S. Andersen*		7.00
____ SECRET POWER OF THE PYRAMIDS *U. S. Andersen*		7.00
____ SELF-THERAPY FOR THE STUTTERER *Malcolm Frazer*		3.00
____ SUCCESS-CYBERNETICS *U. S. Andersen*		7.00
____ 10 DAYS TO A GREAT NEW LIFE *William E. Edwards*		3.00
____ THINK AND GROW RICH *Napoleon Hill*		7.00
____ THINK YOUR WAY TO SUCCESS *Dr. Lew Losoncy*		5.00
____ THREE MAGIC WORDS *U. S. Andersen*		7.00
____ TREASURY OF COMFORT *edited by Rabbi Sidney Greenberg*		5.00
____ TREASURY OF THE ART OF LIVING *Sidney S. Greenberg*		5.00
____ WHAT YOUR HANDWRITING REVEALS *Albert E. Hughes*		3.00
____ YOUR SUBCONSCIOUS POWER *Charles M. Simmons*		7.00
____ YOUR THOUGHTS CAN CHANGE YOUR LIFE *Dr. Donald Curtis*		7.00

SPORTS

____ BICYCLING FOR FUN AND GOOD HEALTH *Kenneth E. Luther*		2.00
____ BILLIARDS—Pocket • Carom • Three Cushion *Clive Cottingham, Jr.*		5.00
____ CAMPING-OUT 101 Ideas & Activities *Bruno Knobel*		2.00
____ COMPLETE GUIDE TO FISHING *Vlad Evanoff*		2.00
____ HOW TO IMPROVE YOUR RACQUETBALL *Lubarsky Kaufman & Scagnetti*		5.00
____ HOW TO WIN AT POCKET BILLIARDS *Edward D. Knuchell*		5.00
____ JOY OF WALKING *Jack Scagnetti*		3.00
____ LEARNING & TEACHING SOCCER SKILLS *Eric Worthington*		3.00
____ MOTORCYCLING FOR BEGINNERS *I. G. Edmonds*		3.00
____ RACQUETBALL FOR WOMEN *Toni Hudson, Jack Scagnetti & Vince Rondone*		3.00
____ RACQUETBALL MADE EASY *Steve Lubarsky, Rod Delson & Jack Scagnetti*		5.00
____ SECRET OF BOWLING STRIKES *Dawson Taylor*		5.00
____ SECRET OF PERFECT PUTTING *Horton Smith & Dawson Taylor*		5.00
____ SOCCER—The Game & How to Play It *Gary Rosenthal*		5.00
____ STARTING SOCCER *Edward F. Dolan, Jr.*		5.00

TENNIS LOVERS' LIBRARY

____ BEGINNER'S GUIDE TO WINNING TENNIS *Helen Hull Jacobs*		2.00
____ HOW TO IMPROVE YOUR TENNIS—Style, Strategy & Analysis *C. Wilson*		2.00
____ PSYCH YOURSELF TO BETTER TENNIS *Dr. Walter A. Luszki*		2.00
____ TENNIS FOR BEGINNERS, *Dr. H. A. Murray*		2.00
____ TENNIS MADE EASY *Joel Brecheen*		4.00
____ WEEKEND TENNIS—How to Have Fun & Win at the Same Time *Bill Talbert*		3.00
____ WINNING WITH PERCENTAGE TENNIS—Smart Strategy *Jack Lowe*		2.00

WILSHIRE PET LIBRARY

____ DOG OBEDIENCE TRAINING *Gust Kessopulos*		5.00
____ DOG TRAINING MADE EASY & FUN *John W. Kellogg*		3.00
____ HOW TO BRING UP YOUR PET DOG *Kurt Unkelbach*		2.00
____ HOW TO RAISE & TRAIN YOUR PUPPY *Jeff Griffen*		5.00

*The books listed above can be obtained from your book dealer or directly from
Melvin Powers. When ordering, please remit $1.00 postage for the first book
and 50¢ for each additional book.*

Melvin Powers
12015 Sherman Road, No. Hollywood, California 91605

HOW TO GET RICH IN MAIL ORDER
by Melvin Powers

Contents:
1. How to Develop Your Mail Order Expertise 2. How to Find a Unique Product or Service to Sell 3. How to Make Money with Classified Ads 4. How to Make Money with Display Ads 5. The Unlimited Potential for Making Money with Direct Mail 6. How to Copycat Successful Mail Order Operations 7. How I Created A Best Seller Using the Copycat Technique 8. How to Start and Run a Profitable Mail Order, Special Interest Book or Record Business 9. I Enjoy Selling Books by Mail—Some of My Successful and Not-So-Successful Ads and Direct Mail Circulars 10. Five of My Most Successful Direct Mail Pieces That Sold and Are Still Selling Millions of Dollars Worth of Books 11. Melvin Powers' Mail Order Success Strategy—Follow It and You'll Become a Millionaire 12. How to Sell Your Products to Mail Order Companies, Retail Outlets, Jobbers, and Fund Raisers for Maximum Distribution and Profits 13. How to Get Free Display Ads and Publicity That Can Put You on the Road to Riches 14. How to Make Your Advertising Copy Sizzle to Make You Wealthy 15. Questions and Answers to Help You Get Started Making Money in Your Own Mail Order Business 16. A Personal Word from Melvin Powers   **8½" x 11" — 352 Pages . . . $21 postpaid**

HOW TO SELF-PUBLISH YOUR BOOK AND HAVE THE FUN AND EXCITEMENT OF BEING A BEST-SELLING AUTHOR
by Melvin Powers

An expert's step-by-step guide to marketing your book successfully

176 Pages . . . $11.00 postpaid

A NEW GUIDE TO RATIONAL LIVING
by Albert Ellis, Ph.D. & Robert A. Harper, Ph.D.

Contents:
1. How Far Can You Go With Self-Analysis? 2. You Feel the Way You Think 3. Feeling Well by Thinking Straight 4. How You Create Your Feelings 5. Thinking Yourself Out of Emotional Disturbances 6. Recognizing and Attacking Neurotic Behavior 7. Overcoming the Influences of the Past 8. Does Reason Always Prove Reasonable? 9. Refusing to Feel Desperately Unhappy 10. Tackling Dire Needs for Approval 11. Eradicating Dire Fears of Failure 12. How to Stop Blaming and Start Living 13. How to Feel Undepressed though Frustrated 14. Controlling Your Own Destiny 15. Conquering Anxiety

256 Pages . . . $7.50 postpaid

PSYCHO-CYBERNETICS
A New Technique for Using Your Subconscious Power
by Maxwell Maltz, M.D., F.I.C.S.

Contents:
1. The Self Image: Your Key to a Better Life 2. Discovering the Success Mechanism Within You 3. Imagination—The First Key to Your Success Mechanism 4. Dehypnotize Yourself from False Beliefs 5. How to Utilize the Power of Rational Thinking 6. Relax and Let Your Success Mechanism Work for You 7. You Can Acquire the Habit of Happiness 8. Ingredients of the Success-Type Personality and How to Acquire Them 9. The Failure Mechanism: How to Make It Work For You Instead of Against You 10. How to Remove Emotional Scars, or How to Give Yourself an Emotional Face Lift 11. How to Unlock Your Real Personality 12. Do-It-Yourself Tranquilizers   **288 Pages . . . $5.50 postpaid**

A PRACTICAL GUIDE TO SELF-HYPNOSIS
by Melvin Powers

Contents:
1. What You Should Know About Self-Hypnosis 2. What About the Dangers of Hypnosis? 3. Is Hypnosis the Answer? 4. How Does Self-Hypnosis Work? 5. How to Arouse Yourself from the Self-Hypnotic State 6. How to Attain Self-Hypnosis 7. Deepening the Self-Hypnotic State 8. What You Should Know About Becoming an Excellent Subject 9. Techniques for Reaching the Somnambulistic State 10. A New Approach to Self-Hypnosis When All Else Fails 11. Psychological Aids and Their Function 12. The Nature of Hypnosis 13. Practical Applications of Self-Hypnosis   **128 Pages . . . $3.50 postpaid**

The books listed above can be obtained from your book dealer or directly from Melvin Powers.

Melvin Powers
12015 Sherman Road, No. Hollywood, California 91605